HOME AGAIN
Preparing International Students to Serve Christ in their Home Country

Nate Mirza

The Navigators
International Student Ministry
P.O. Box 6000
Colorado Springs, CO 80934

Association of Christian
Ministries to Internationals
P. O. Box 4050
Spring, TX 77380

Printed in the United States of America

To Gerry O. De Young
my spiritual father
who taught me to follow Christ
as a young international student believer

CONTENTS

ACKNOWLEDGMENTS 7
INTRODUCTION 9
1 FACING REALITY
   Stories of Disaster, Delight, and Debriefing 13
2 WHO IS AT MY DOORSTEP?
   *The Mind-set of Internationals Coming to Study in the
   United States* 17
3 BECOMING AMERICAN
   How International Students Change 19
4 IS THIS HOME?
   What Graduates Face Upon Returning Home 23
5 LAYING THE FOUNDATION
   *Preparing Internationals Before Leaving the Host
   Country* 37
6 BUILDING THE SUPERSTRUCTURE
   Priority Issues of Reentry Preparation 47
7 VISITING THE INTERNATIONAL
   A Unique Commitment as a Spiritual Parent 77
8 HOME AGAIN
   Help Available in Home Countries 81
9 CONCLUSION 85
   APPENDIX A
   *Organizations with Opportunities Abroad for International
   Graduates* 87
   APPENDIX B
   Tips on Traveling to Visit Returnees 89
   APPENDIX C
   *Recommended Books, Videos, and Audio Tapes for
   Returning Internationals* 93
   APPENDIX D
   Other Resource Materials on Reentry 97

ACKNOWLEDGMENTS

I am first and foremost indebted to my Savior, the Lord Jesus Christ, for having mercifully drawn me to Himself through various channels. These included my parents as well as American and international Christians whom I met while I was a foreign student from Iran studying at Cal Poly, San Luis Obispo, California.

I also wish to express deep gratitude to all those international students, both Christian and not yet Christian, who taught me so much about ministry. They have instructed, modeled, challenged, and molded my understanding and modus operandi.

A great debt of gratitude is due a number of men and women of various cultures, churches, and Christian organizations who very helpfully critiqued various drafts of this manuscript. They are worthy of being named: Wilson Awasu, Tom and Stacey Bieler, David Bok, Leiton and Lisa-Espineli Chinn, Mike and Judie Crouse, Hal Guffey, Paul and Margaret Hensley, Samir Husni, Kok Leng Khew, Lawson Lau, Meri McLeod, Phil Saksa, Don Simpson, Jean Stephens, Hui-Ming Wee, Tom Yeakley, and those endorsing the book. For the unintentional errors and weaknesses in this book, I take full responsibility.

Without the secretarial assistance of Phyllis Nielsen, I would still be working on the manuscript. I am very grateful to Jeff

Stoddard for excellent artwork and Chandran Mannar who took care of the color separation for the cover. My thanks extends also to several people at NavPress for invaluable advice and help. Finally, to Ben Hanna for the layout work done in such a cheerful manner.

For much of this book I am obligated to the aforementioned, as well as to a wonderful band of dedicated, loving people ministering to internationals who network with each other through the Association of Christian Ministries to Internationals (ACMI).

May the Lord multiply them and the fruit of their labors around the world to help bring to the full number those who are being redeemed by our blessed Savior, "men from every tribe and language and people and nation."

INTRODUCTION

From Genesis to Revelation, God's heart beats for people. He had individuals in mind long before they were born (Psalm 139:11-18). He was Adam and Eve's constant companion in a relationship of holiness and perfection. Even when they fell into sin, God's love for them was so great that He humbled Himself and took the initiative to redeem them, calling out to Adam, "Where are you?" (Genesis 3:9).

His plan for the redemption of all men included the promise to Abraham that through him "all peoples on earth will be blessed" (Genesis 12:3). His strategy was to develop a nation that would so exemplify Him and His righteous government that other nations would be attracted to Him. When Israel failed in this task, He chose a new people, the Church, to represent Him by going "to the ends of the earth" (Acts 1:8).

I like to think of Acts 2:1-12 as God's "Headstart Program." Since the commission was to go to the Gentile world, God gave the Church a flying start by having pilgrims representing some fourteen language groups (Parthians, Medes, Elamites, Egyptians, Libyans, Romans, Cretans, Arabs, among others) in Jerusalem at the same time to hear Peter preach the good news of salvation through Jesus Christ. Many turned to Christ and took the gospel back to their own people.

In a parallel way God is bringing the representatives of the nations, as university students, scholars, special trainees, business people, and military and diplomatic personnel, to places like Australia, Canada, England, France, India, New Zealand, and the United States. In these countries, where the gospel can be freely proclaimed, they have the opportunity of turning to Christ, going back to their people, and helping them turn to the Lord.

The vision of this worldwide missions strategy is clear, the logic is compelling, the advantages are obvious, and the potential is motivating. But does it work? Indeed it does and it has. Are there pitfalls? Certainly. Don't all strategies carried out by humans have pitfalls? In this book I am concerned about the very real pitfall of international believers returning to their home countries and not being effective laborers for Jesus Christ.

What are these pitfalls? What do the returnees face upon returning? There is much written about reentry from a secular as well as a Christian perspective. "Reentry" has become a technical term referring to what people who have lived for some time in a culture other than their own experience upon returning to their own culture. This book is designed to help you develop a discipleship orientation and expose you to appropriate resources to prepare international students for this reentry. What can those of us involved in discipling them do to reduce the number of dropouts and increase the quality and quantity of Christ-centered laborers? If they don't keep walking with God and labor in His name among the nations, then the vision of discipling internationals is not being fulfilled.

While the primary audience I am addressing are those discipling international Christians, the students themselves will profit from reading the material. Many of them have national student fellowships in their universities and would welcome the opportunity to use this information in their meetings.

One issue calls for clarification. In this work no attempt has been made to differentiate between graduates and undergraduates. However, one critique of the original manuscript included the following insightful comments by Lawson Lau, author of *The World at Your Doorstep*: "Statistics show that international students are about evenly divided between undergraduates and graduates. While there are a lot of similarities between these groups, the graduate student is often more mature than the undergraduate, if we take it that the undergraduate is usually much younger than the graduate student. The dynamics are also somewhat different for those who are married and have children. There is greater stability although the impact of change on their children is even more significant."

The driving force behind this book is not so much to propound an attractive strategy for reaching foreigners outside their own culture, nor to tap the potential these future leaders of the nations have. It is the vision that God loves the people of all nations, that He is developing an intracultural Kingdom made up of people growing in holiness and righteousness, that He alone is to be glorified, that He works in answer to prayer, and that He graciously uses us as we cooperate with His strategies.

My desire in writing this book is to somehow contribute to the fulfillment of Revelation 15:3-4:

Great and marvelous are your deeds,
Lord God Almighty.
Just and true are your ways,
King of the ages.
Who will not fear you, O Lord,
and bring glory to your name?
For you alone are holy.
All nations will come
and worship before you,
for your righteous acts have been revealed.

1
FACING REALITY
Stories of Disaster, Delight, and Debriefing

✜

 " I am committed to marry this girl, no matter who says what."
His parents were against it, the church people were against it,
the Bible was against it, and I certainly couldn't support it. But
Budi was determined.

Budi had been sent to study in the United States by an agency
of his government. After about two years of close contact with
Christians and considerable Bible investigation, he turned to Christ
as his Lord and Savior. Over the next two and a half years, he
showed many signs of the new life—including changed attitudes,
habits, and values; an increased desire for God and His Word and
for ministering to others; attendance at conferences, training
programs, and church; and the demonstration of good stewardship.

Upon returning to his country after graduation, he was not able
to get a job in his field of study and began training in another field.
He made contact with believers and became actively involved in a
church and Bible study. However, the unusual hours required by
his job made it more and more difficult to participate in the
fellowship of the church and Bible-study groups. He met a woman
at work who was not a believer. After marrying her, he had no
desire to follow and serve the Lord. This brought great heartache
to his family, friends, and God.

All the vision, prayer, work, and hopes of seeing him being used by God among his own people seem shattered. Of course, the last chapter has not yet been written. God has not given up. Each time I go to Budi's city, I call him to assure him of my love and prayers.

Budi's case is illustrative of the potential pitfalls facing international graduates when they return home. One group of Asian Christians, who were actively involved in their American campus ministry in Oregon, returned home and decided they had done their "Christian thing" at the university and now it was time to give themselves to making money.

Fortunately, scores of stories can be told about international students who have returned and been significantly used by God in ministry to their own people. Lin Su is active in outreach at Korea University. Hiroshi teaches mathematics in a university in Japan and is involved in student ministry and his local church. Mutuwa is the director of the Kenya Navigators. Wee has been a university professor outside his country, discipling students. John influenced a whole denomination in Malaysia with the concept and practice of discipleship. Rocky, who built a furniture factory in Indonesia, has provided jobs for people and is seeing some of them come to Christ. Johnny reached out to people at a major bank in Jakarta. Danielo, Nitya, and Sonia are doing Bible translation work with Wycliffe Bible Translators in Indonesia. Abraham has established a mission group in India that is planting churches among people of Hindu background. Johnny leads a parachurch movement in Malaysia. Emmanuel is a university researcher and part-time evangelist in Tanzania. William is a pastor and past-president of his denomination in Ghana. Peter is a layman ministering to street children and their parents in Singapore. And the list goes on.

Preparing international students for effective ministry is not easy. The purpose of this book is twofold: to provide understanding of reentry realities for those discipling international students; and to point to some strategies that will better prepare the returning graduates to reintegrate into their cultures harmoniously and effectively as disciples and servants of Jesus Christ.

The size of this book does not allow me to be culture-specific. However, our best teachers in learning the specifics of each culture we are dealing with are the students and scholars themselves. We must become their students. Nor do I want to think of international students in a homogeneous fashion. While my experience is primarily with Asians, my desire is to share principles that will generically help those assisting internationals with reentry. There is no substitute for visiting various countries and learning firsthand what the internationals face upon returning home.

2
WHO IS AT MY DOORSTEP?

The Mind-set of Internationals Coming to Study in the United States

What is the mind-set of university students coming to the United States for a degree? Generally, the following desires and characteristics are present:

- To excel in their studies, which requires significant cultural change.
- To not disappoint their parents.
- To benefit their country through their profession.
- To position themselves in high places of government, education, the military, business, or industry back home in order to enjoy the resultant power, prestige, and money.
- To hold on to their traditions, values, and religion.
- To see well-known places like the White House, Disneyland, the Grand Canyon, etc.

Some intend to stay and live the "good life" in the United States. Others do not like the U.S. They disagree with its politics and culture and are resentful of its influential role in international affairs. All they want is the advantage of a Western degree. For instance, while many of the almost ten thousand Iranians studying in the land of "the Great Satan" may not appreciate much about the

17

United States, they appreciate the value of an American degree and education.

Before coming here, the students' picture of the U.S. is primarily influenced by seeing Hollywood movies and supplemented by reading comics and magazines and hearing anecdotes. One group of students in an English class at the Baptist College in Hong Kong said the first thing that came to their mind when thinking of the U.S. was crime and sex. Movies have conditioned them to expect a country of tall buildings, crime, and blondes!

3
BECOMING AMERICAN
How International Students Change
✚

Over a period of two to seven years of study in the United States, a gradual and often nondiscernable change takes place in the outlook, values, and habits of international students. While they will admit to some changes, they often have no idea how profound these changes have been. They don't even realize some of the changes that have occurred. The person who came to study is not the same one returning with a degree. What contributes to this metamorphosis?

1. Experiencing the normal process of maturing that takes place between the ages of eighteen and twenty-four. This involves a greater degree of independence, sometimes a rebellion against values they were raised with, and the development of values of their own.

2. Eagerly expecting to learn new things. In most cases, America is looked on as more advanced than their own countries. Those students with patriotic goals expect to apply what they learn in the U.S. to the advancement of their home countries. Therefore, to become Americanized is very desirable in areas of technology, dress, music, etc.

3. Changing from a social and educational system where they are accustomed to being fed information to one where they are encouraged to be critical, evaluate, or discover for themselves.

Many will come from political systems where the press, books, and movies are censored and where the national media is government controlled. For example, for years you could not see the movie *Ben Hur* in Arab countries. Other countries ban books on Communism.

4. Crossing the ocean brings with it the lifting of parental restrictions. They observe what appears to them to be very undisciplined American students indulging in alcohol, drugs, sex, heavily sex-oriented movies, abusive language, pornographic literature, broken family relationships, and lack of respect for the elderly. While international students have come to the campus for an education, it seems their American counterparts have a lot of time for fun and recreation. While they were not immune to any of this in their home countries, the unrestricted access and open display of this lifestyle, while shocking at first, are gradually assimilated.

Over the years, changes will take place in these students. Some will become more aggressive, demanding, and critical; others will learn to work harder than they used to. Some will start to express themselves more openly without regard to their "place in society." Many will become more independent and individualistic; and some will consider cross-cultural marriage.

All this impacts the reentry experience. In the early days after their return they may be full of negative responses, criticism, and frustration toward their home country. The locals interpret these as pride, arrogance, and a feeling of superiority on the part of the returnees. They in turn do not feel accepted, leaving them with three choices: to turn around and go back to the States; to seek out the comfort of the foreign-graduate subculture; or to humbly die to themselves, letting their people be their teachers and seeking to serve them. The latter attitude can only be achieved by the power of Christ and in response to a higher vision than material prosperity and personal psychological well-being.

A fact of life is that "third-culture" people will probably never be able to be completely at home in their indigenous culture, nor fully at home in the culture in which they gained their higher education. But this needs to be seen as a potential asset rather than a liability. The blatant expressions of evil can be seen and rejected. The free atmosphere to think, evaluate, and believe differently can lead them to the truth of Christ. The hard work can be channeled in godly directions, bearing eternal fruit in the lives of others. The ability to make money can benefit their families, the poor, and the work of God's Kingdom.

However, the more Americanized a student becomes, the more difficult the adjustment when he or she returns home. Inevitable clashes will occur between the values of the Americanized returnee, who has in fact become a third-culture person, and those of the people in the home culture.

4

IS THIS HOME?

What Graduates Face Upon Returning Home

At one international-student conference, I asked a group of students what their fears and anxieties were about going home after graduation.[1] Their worries included:

- How people back home would respond to their speaking their own language with a foreign accent. In some cases, they will have forgotten some of their own language.
- Facing parental authority after being independent for so long.
- A feeling of alienation due to a change of values, ideas, and ways of thinking compared to those of their parents and former friends. The inability to express these to those at home, to be understood, and still to be accepted, adds to the anxiety.
- Possible marriage arrangements.
- Incompatibility with the old culture.
- Fear of rejection because they have changed so much.
- Uncertainty about whether to go back, since they like the quality of life in the United States.

Marconi received both his bachelor's and master's degrees in the United States. When I saw him in Jakarta, he was looking for a job. He expressed the following observations about himself and other returnees:

1. There is a tendency to feel what we have learned abroad is superior and, therefore, to look down on those who study at home.
2. People here look up to foreign graduates and therefore feed that sense of superiority.
3. By expressing myself too frankly, I hurt people here.
4. I constantly compare Indonesia with the United States and complain about Indonesia.
5. In the United States I learned to encourage other people. People don't do that in Indonesia.
6. In the United States I developed an individualistic mentality that makes it hard to fit into a culture with group orientation.
7. I struggle with the lack of privacy.
8. It's important to learn to solve problems, not just sweep them under the rug.
9. After being in the States I have a greater appreciation for servants (domestic help) in Indonesia.
10. It is helpful to learn to agree to disagree while in the United States. Here disagreement is equated with enmity or being against the person.

ADJUSTING TO THE HOME COUNTRY

What will international students face when they return home? Chandran, an Indian from Singapore, graduated from Oklahoma State University. The first thing that struck him upon returning was the heat and humidity. He found himself taking three or four showers a day! He was frustrated with his lower energy level. He couldn't do as much as he did in Stillwater. He was tempted to complain about this, but it would only have encouraged a negative attitude toward other areas of his life. It took him about three months to reaccept the humidity as a fact of life.

Other readjustments international students will face upon their return home include the following.

Traffic

After several years of living where relatively orderly traffic stays in marked lanes, stepping into a megacity like Jakarta or Manila feels chaotic. An endless stream of cars, motorcycles, and other vehicles—all with horns blaring and tailpipes spewing pollution—vying for inches of space to get ahead can be nerve-racking.

Health and Hygiene

The average American has been taught that "cleanliness is next to godliness." The health department meticulously inspects super-markets and restaurants. You don't find flies feasting on cuts of meat at grocery stores like Safeway. But in many parts of the world, a side of lamb will hang in the open air off a busy street along which open drains may run. For someone who has become used to the former, revulsion to the latter is understandable. For the returnee, having become accustomed to higher standards of hygiene, it is tempting to compare and criticize, giving the impression to the local people that this graduate of an American university feels superior to them.

Public Services

International students in the United States get used to fairly courteous, friendly, and reasonably prompt treatment at the post office, campus administration building, or driver's license office. The notable exception is the dreaded Immigration and Naturalization Service (INS), because it has the power to deport them from the United States, thus frustrating their educational goals. To them the INS is what the former Russian secret police (KGB) was to Americans. But generally speaking, public and private services are courteous and friendly with minimum red tape.

Returning home to find that you have to elbow your way to the post-office counter and hand your letters to the clerk around the neck of the person in front of you...well, it's an adjustment. To walk into a government office and see the official with a newspaper on his desk and seemingly nothing else to do, yet he won't acknowledge your presence or ask, "How may I help you?" but keeps you waiting while he sips tea and chats with his friends …well, it's another adjustment. After a number of experiences like these, the returnee, besides complaining and criticizing, is tempted to think, *I don't have to put up with this. I think I'll just go back to Madison, Wisconsin. I'll trade their winters for this any day!* I don't know how many returnees I've heard say, "After the first week back home, I was ready to get on a plane and go right back to the States."

Work/Career

After graduation, getting a job is the graduate's main concern. "Will I find a job in my field? How long will it take? How many times will I be turned down? Will my parents be proud of the job I get?" Chandran looked eight months before finding a job in Singapore. On the other hand, Marconi had about eight job offers within a few weeks in Indonesia, each with more attractive benefits than the previous one. John's degree in geology wasn't useful during the oil industry slump of the early 1980s, so he ended up becoming an air-traffic controller. Subconsciously, some U.S. graduates think of themselves as elitists for whom companies should roll out the red carpet at the airport and offer top jobs. It is a great blow to their ego when the job-hunting process goes on for what seems an eternity. Often, they view themselves as failures.

The graduate faces other challenges in the marketplace as well, like whether he or she should go after government or private-sector jobs. In most countries the working week is five and a half days. But even in overseas settings, most American companies work on a five-day basis. Often government jobs offer no challenge. In Oman graduates like government jobs because they finish by 2:00 p.m., leaving time to carry on with private businesses where they make their real money.

The graduate also must confront corruption, bribery, and deceit. For Christian students with a sensitive conscience this area is very painful. On one hand, the word in the marketplace is, "You cannot do business here without bribing." On the other hand, the Bible teaches, "Now let the fear of the Lord be upon you. Judge carefully, for with the Lord our God there is no injustice or partiality or bribery" (2 Chronicles 19:7), and "A wicked man accepts a bribe in secret to pervert the course of justice" (Proverbs 17:23). The Holy Spirit tells them that bribery is displeasing to God.

Consider this scenario. The returnee's company needs an export license from the government. The returnee presents a government official with the appropriate application form, and the official puts the application document under the large pile on his desk and tells the returnee to come back in a week. The returnee knows very well that if an envelope with some money is attached to the document, the job will get done right away. After all, the official has eight children whom he cannot feed and educate on his paltry government salary. The returnee's mind is in high gear, thinking, *Is it worth waiting a week? This license is worth millions in foreign exchange. It will benefit the company, the country's trade balance, and perhaps get me a bonus. Besides, if I come back in a week, the official could say the boss was on vacation and won't be back for another week. Or a new person might be on the job. Or the document may get lost. If I give him money, am I asking him to "pervert the course of justice," or am I merely encouraging him to do what he should do?*

I have known sincere believers to come down on both sides of this question. Some will not pay, believing it to be a bribe. Others will pay, believing they are not breaking any law, but merely helping the official do what he's supposed to do.

The pressures of the marketplace; the universal problems of interpersonal conflicts; the problem of colleagues taking advantage of their diligence and hard work; and being passed over for promotions and being discriminated against on the job because they don't belong to the right religion, family, or ethnic group —these factors can seriously tempt the returnees to look for easier alternatives. Their vision of being salt and light and spreading the fragrant aroma of Christ in the workplace is severely tested.

Another problem Christian job hunters face is balancing work and ministry. The returnee must ask himself or herself the following questions: What are my motivations for wanting this job? Are they money, prestige, power, professional challenge, ministry opportunity? What is the price to be paid for a good job?

When is the price too high? In Malaysia, Cheng leaves home at 6:30 a.m. and returns at 8:30 p.m. With at least an hour's bus ride on each end, one may ask if it is worth it. Does he have another choice? Can God create a better opportunity in answer to believing prayer? Should Cheng do this for a couple of years to gain work experience and then be more choosy?

Khew, a Malaysian Christian highly committed to ministry and a graduate from an Australian university, speaks of the "rubber band effect." When career and ministry are stretched to the limit, one of them has to give. Which one will it be? Khew is convinced that if God is put first He will bless His servants in the area of work with such rewards as promotions. This, of course, is not necessarily always true.

Also, at what level of affluence does God want me to live? All over the world the pull of materialism is strong. Parents pressure their children to earn lots of money and gain a high position in society, partly because it reflects well on them. One father gave his newly returned son a gold-colored Mercedes Benz.

Khew, who worked for Hewlett-Packard in Kuala Lumpur for ten years, addresses the affluence issue by saying, "The issue is not the high cost of living but the cost of high living. It is so easy to live beyond our means, but the challenge is to give beyond our means." The insights he has gained from struggling with these issues may help others struggling with discipleship commitments.

The questions raised above do not have easy answers. Individuals have to make choices specifically sensitive to their context after seeking God and His Word and counseling with His people. We should not judge them if their choice differs from our opinion, but rather encourage them to keep walking with God, working hard, and trusting God for changes in the workplace. Romans 14, the first part of 15, and 1 Corinthians 8, 9, and 10 are very helpful chapters to study on making decisions on issues that are not clearly right or wrong.

Family Expectations

In most non-Western societies, families are the glue of society. Hierarchy, leadership, and authority structures are respected even if the relationships are not close. Extended families are interdependent. Some older children will forgo a college education in order to work to provide the younger siblings with higher education. Those with degrees are expected to help with the education of younger ones. Parents can insist on the returned son or daughter working for the family business. Often in Chinese societies, the father's role is to provide materially and give orders that he expects to be obeyed. Close relationships where there is the freedom to talk about dreams, desires, plans, feelings, and views are rare.

Place back into this context a son who has learned to be an independent individualist over several years of being abroad, and you have great potential for conflict in the family. He has been making his own decisions, choosing his own convictions, and making his own time commitments as a result of turning to Christ or simply living in the United States.

In Islamic, Hindu, Jewish, and Chinese cultures, religion and culture and nationhood are so inextricably entwined that turning to Christ is often interpreted as betrayal of culture, family, and nationality. It becomes incumbent on a believer to be very sensitive to honoring father and mother in every way possible while not violating a biblically based conscience before God.

Once again Khew, who is married and has two children, has been very helpful with practical insights, especially in the Chinese setting, for dealing with family expectations. His suggestions follow:

FAMILY EXPECTATIONS	RESPONSE
■ They want to see you.	Go to parents' home for lunch once a week.
■ They look for gifts from you.	Give cash regularly in small amounts. On birthdays and Chinese New Year, give larger amounts. Bring home small gifts and treats now and then. Love is expressed more in deeds than words in the Asian context.
■ If you live at home, you'll be treated as a child.	If you move out and visit your parents, you'll be treated as a guest.
■ If you live at home, the development of your spiritual life will be limited.	You have more control of how you conduct your spiritual life when you are able to live on your own.

FAMILY EXPECTATIONS	RESPONSE
■ Participation in religious customs.	With humility, make your stand for Christ known early. The longer you wait, the harder it is. See *How to Speak to Our Elders About Christ*, on page 64.

Friendships

Time does not stand still; neither do friends. Subconsciously, international students will expect to return and pick up with their high school or college friends where they left off several years earlier. This is often not the case. The friends have had at least four years to make other friends. Old friendships have drifted apart due to lack of contact, changing locations, or marriage. Once married, many seek friendships with other married couples instead of maintaining friendships with singles. When I visited Seah in Singapore about nine months after he had returned, he told me that he had to start making friends all over again. This is a common experience among returnees.

These realities make it imperative that we introduce Christian internationals to fellow believers from their country, even if this has to be done on a statewide, regional, or even nationwide basis in their country of study. Once they return, they will have each other for encouragement, challenge, and support. An illustration of a national forum is the Post-Urbana Missionary Convention International Conference, held every three years at the University of Illinois. Here students of like nationality have discovered each other for the first time as believers. Many have expressed deep gratitude for this.

Marriage

The two areas of life on the top of parents' concerns for their grown children are *financial security* and *marriage*. How will the children support themselves, as well as their parents? Will the children have a happy married life that will reflect well on the parents and the family name?

Sending the children abroad for a university education is designed to meet the first need. The second need is often being worked on while the children are abroad. Parents, grandparents, and other relatives are on the lookout for prospects. Their first choice is someone from the same race.

Bee, a Malaysian Chinese, married David, a South Indian, in the United States, much to the displeasure of her parents. Because of prayer, correspondence, and their visit to her home country, the parents gradually accepted the groom and gave their blessing.

Returning women are under much greater pressure in the area of marriage than men. What does the Christian woman do when her parents want her to marry a nonbeliever? Does she take a stand on not being "unequally yoked"? Does she surrender to her parents' wishes in order to please them and not create tension, thinking this is honoring her parents? What principles and convictions are going to help her make such decisions? What are the real issues being faced? Is she honoring father and mother? Is she submitting to the lordship of Christ? Is she trusting God that He can do the seemingly impossible in changing her parents' attitudes or providing a believing husband?

An encouraging example is the story of a Malaysian girl from a Hindu family who had come to faith in Christ. She prayed for a believing husband. In her case, the cultural norm was for the parents to choose the husband, even if she had never met him. Unknown to the parents or their daughter, they chose a man from a Hindu family who had also come to Christ while studying abroad.

Discovering that they each loved the Lord, they married, thankful that God had answered their prayers. Twelve years and three children later, they continue to have a loving family and exemplary relationship with Christ.

Spiritual Life

International students come with a variety of religious or spiritual backgrounds—nominal adherents, devout believers, or of no formal religious background; seekers or rejecters of religion; uninterested in or bitter toward God; or simply curious. Depending on the intensity of the change after coming to Christ while abroad, the implications hold varying degrees of seriousness. The attitude of the parents to a spiritual change in their children will be an important issue. Two Malaysian sisters told me that before leaving home, their Buddhist mother gave them strict instructions not to become Christians and not to marry Americans. So far they have not married Americans!

When a Muslim, a Jew, a Hindu, or a Buddhist turns to Christ, he or she usually considers the consequences very carefully first. When a Muslim converts, he or she will be accused of committing the sin of apostasy (which can be punishable by death). Once the conversion is known in the community, the reputation of the family becomes a major issue. The student may be disinherited, be evicted from home, be discriminated against in the job market, or even face the possibility of being put to death. A decision for Christ does not come easily or carelessly.

Think about an international woman who turns to Christ while abroad with no Christian roots of church, friends, or Bible-study group to go back to. The style of worship and church life and the way in which Christian men and women fellowship with each other abroad could be a problem when she returns to her country, where she has to face very different patterns in the Christian community. Some churches in Japan have the reputation of being very legalistic about their do's and don'ts. A Japanese student who came to Christ in a freer church setting finds difficulty in handling the new situation at home.

This creates a greater need for the discipler to become familiar with what the church and Christian community are like in the home context. Sources for such information would include believers from that country who live here, missionaries who have served in the country, or mission agencies who have ministries there. Thus, our biblical teaching should emphasize principles, which can then be adapted to a given culture. Attitudes become crucial. Patience, listening carefully to why things are done in a particular way at home, and humility when there are honest differences will make the readjustment process less traumatic.

While international believers are in the States, they are often the object of a lot of attention from other internationals or Americans. They feel loved, accepted, nurtured, affirmed, and trained. Their social and spiritual needs are met in the international fellowship. They are a minority that was fussed over. When they return home they become a part of the majority, with little or no fuss made over them. The same warm spiritual family is no longer there. They feel alone, abandoned, uncared for. To make spiritual progress, they must have strong convictions or take a lot of initiative toward other believers to become part of a new spiritual family. Those who don't invariably stop following or growing in Christ.

This points to two implications on the part of disciplers: (1) the importance of visiting them soon after they return and personally introducing them to local believers, and (2) the development of good relationships with God's people in the home country to facilitate the adoption of the new believer into God's family there.

Habits and Customs

We learn both by spontaneous assimilation from our dominant culture and by cognitive learning. The former has a deeper impact on our behavior than the latter because it has developed from childhood on. While some habits or customs may be lost while in an alien culture, after returning it's mainly a matter of time before these dominant behavior patterns return. Dr. Appianda Arthur of Ghana tells that in his country one does not point at other people with the left hand. When a Ghanian lives in the United States several years, where pointing with either hand is common, he can unconsciously absorb the new custom. But back in Ghana, it will only take a few stares or perhaps outright correction by offended people before he will go back to his natural custom.

Some of the more common American habits that international students assimilate include:

- Chewing gum.
- Sitting in a slouched rather than an upright manner.
- Hugging (most Asians don't hug each other in Asia).
- Wearing very informal clothing, like shorts and singlets.
- Dating the opposite sex.

The more foreign the new habits of the returnees, the less acceptable they are to their fellow countrymen. This form of rejection makes the reintegration process that much more difficult.

Attitude

Due to past experience, people in the home countries expect the foreign graduate (of American universities, especially) to return with an attitude of pride, arrogance, and superiority. Returning graduates can be vitriolic about what they don't like at home as they measure what they are seeing and experiencing with what took place in the U.S., Canada, Australia, or England. This attitude makes their readjustment to the home culture much more problematic.

It is at the level of one's spirit that the greatest difficulty or greatest potential for good lies. A know-it-all attitude does not bode well for healthy relationships with peers, neighbors, or relatives. An independent attitude communicates to parents that they are not respected anymore, causing them to wonder if the thousands of dollars invested was a waste. An attitude that criticizes everything local and praises everything foreign causes people to want to distance themselves from the returnee.

SUMMARY

The reentry process is difficult for many international students because they have to make major adjustments in many areas all at the same time. It is not a matter of dealing with the weather, then facing the parental challenge, and once that is under control, dealing with the career issue. It just doesn't work that way. The problems are piled one on top of another. No wonder that within the first few weeks some are seriously tempted to catch the next jumbo jet back to the United States. Little or nothing in their university experience has prepared them to face these challenges.

In time the superficial adjustments to such matters as weather, customs, and food are made, but more profound inner changes like philosophy, values, and attitudes stay with the third-culture person and produce both conflicts as well as vehicles for being positive change agents.

How can international students be better prepared to return home and cope with the inevitable stresses of adjustment? How can the potential for being change agents be developed under the control of the Holy Spirit? That is what the next chapter will deal with.

NOTE

1. See also "Potential Reentry Problems" in *Think Home* (see Appendix D).

5
LAYING
THE FOUNDATION

*Preparing Internationals
Before Leaving the Host Country*

✜

Given an understanding of what graduates face upon returning home, how can those who are discipling the international students plan their ministry to better prepare them for these experiences? Though the suggested strategy that follows is offered with Christian internationals in mind, many nonChristians will also appreciate the insights, for they too will face similar realities of reentry. In fact, the subject can often lead naturally into their need for a right relationship with God.

FOUNDATIONS

Christ-centeredness
Our first step in laying proper foundations for reentry is to ensure that our international friends who have *Jesus Christ living in them* are secure in their assurance of salvation (Romans 10:9-10), forgiveness of sins (Ephesians 1:7), acceptance by God as His children (John 1:12-13), and possessing eternal life (1 John 5:11-13).

A second step is to help believers develop a *growing relationship with Christ*—both as the very essence of their life (Galatians 2:20, Colossians 3:1-4) and as the object of their life

37

(Philippians 1:20-21). No one else is worthy of living and dying for, therefore we want to help them get to know the Savior and experience Him living His life in and through them (Galatians 2:20). Certain spiritual disciplines are necessary for growth, but they are not an end in themselves. They are the means by which we get to know Him, become more like Him, and learn to serve Him gladly.

The Bible
The Bible is God's primary means through which He makes Himself and His will known to us (Hebrews 1:1-3). We must help our friends learn to feed on God's Word for themselves, so that they will not fall when they are alone because they have become too dependent on others. Chapter 6 of this book offers some suggested materials to help international students get into the Bible.

When choosing materials, the following questions would be useful to ask:

- Are the materials suitable for the student's level of English? Are they available in his or her language?
- Can the materials be used once the student returns to his or her country?
- Do the materials communicate Western ways of learning (analysis, conceptualization) that might be foreign to the student's culture?
- Are these materials faithful to the message of the Bible as a whole?
- Can they easily be taught to others?
- Are they affordable?

If you cannot find appropriate materials, ask God for the inspiration to create your own. Don't be hampered by a lack of materials. The apostles didn't have any. The church in China didn't have any, yet it grew from 700,000 to about 50 million in one generation when Bibles were scarce and pastors imprisoned. You can always go through the Bible book by book. That's the way God's revelation came.

One universal need is to have an overview of the Bible, coupled with a study on the inspiration and authority of Scripture. This can help develop bedrock, lifelong convictions that will help students stand in any situation. A Bible handbook such as Unger's or Halley's will be useful in meeting this need. Charts and maps in study Bibles like the *New International Version* are also helpful. Because the Old Testament is an unknown quantity to people with a nonChristian background, students appreciate being guided through it.

Our goal should include developing a love for the Scriptures so that international students will make them a normal lifelong part of their lives. Mr. K. gets up at 5:00 a.m. in Jakarta to make sure he gets adequate time with God before going into a fierce business world. He is living by conviction, not by convenience. Do we demonstrate that to our international friends?

Prayer

Prayer is communication with God during which we confess sin, worship, and thank God, expressing our deepest thoughts, desires, disappointments, and intercessions to Him. In prayer we can respond to what He has been saying to us in the Bible. We can surrender our struggles to His will. We can consciously turn to Him at any time of day or night, in any place and any position, and express our love for Him and our dependence on Him (Ephesians 6:18-19). Without a consistent prayer life of listening to the "still, small voice," the mounting pressures of life will not be withstood victoriously. The light will not shine and the salt will lose its taste. International students must see a lifestyle of prayer exemplified in our lives, study what the Bible says about it, learn to practice it, and be exposed to praying people.

Obedience

Obedience is God's chosen key to a greater knowledge of Christ (John 14:21,23) and spiritual maturity (Hebrews 5:11-14). By example and teaching we must show international students how to put into practice what God says in the Bible based on our love for Christ. This may involve changing attitudes and behavior in relationships, habits, priorities, what we feed our minds, or how we serve Him. This is how we "put off [our] old self…and…put on the new self" (Ephesians 4:22-24).

Interdependence

Interdependence within the Body of Christ is the recognition that when Jesus saved us, He placed us into a body of believers. He prayed that we would be united, and planned that each part of the Body would work in harmonious interdependence to fulfill His evangelistic (John 17:21) and Christian maturity (Ephesians 4:11-16) purposes.

Interdependence is found in one-to-one relationships, small discipleship groups, house churches, larger churches, and world-level conferences. International students will face the pressures of their reentry experience far more constructively when they link up with men and women of like vision and commitment in the home country. Graduate fellowships exist in various countries for such purposes. In Indonesia a group called *The Marketplace Ministry* receives returnees and provides support, encouragement, and training where needed.

At a recent Indonesian Christian conference I was asked why so many believers who were on fire for the Lord while in the States backslid when home and no longer followed the Lord. This is a painful fact. One reason is because once they returned they did not join other Christians who could encourage and help them.

While we cannot guarantee a returnee's choices upon returning, we can minimize the attrition rate by asking ourselves questions like the following:

- Is the spirit and content of our international fellowships here merely meeting social needs?
- Are we actually teaching what biblical fellowship is?
- Are we making a concerted effort to connect those soon to return with believers in their countries who will reach out to them?
- Do we discuss with those about to return such issues as the temptations they expect to encounter back home; the divine and human resources they can call on to overcome

these temptations; and how soon after returning they plan
to get in touch with believers?
■ Do we pray with them about these matters?

Both the material below and that in chapter 6 attempts to
provide a context in which these questions are dealt with.

Evangelism

Evangelism is to the believer as farming is to the farmer, or
running to the runner. Jesus commissioned His followers to be His
witnesses to the ends of the earth (Acts 1:8). The Apostle Paul's
stated ambition was "to preach the gospel where Christ was not
known" (Romans 15:20). It is a fact that where evangelism
decreases or is not practiced, spiritual life fades away.

Some questions we should ask ourselves as we prepare
international students in this foundation include:

1. Do we let the international students see our practice of
    evangelism in natural as well as planned ways?
2. Have we trained them so they have confidence in sharing
    the good news of Christ with others?
3. Have we discussed the specific social structures of the
    people they could witness to once they return, such as
    immediate family, extended family, the rich, the laborer
    class, and the poor? What parallel situations can we
    expose them to here to better prepare them? If it is the
    workplace, have we introduced them to people in the
    working world who have a credible witness to their
    colleagues? Might the inner city or an ethnic community
    be an appropriate training context?

The graduates coming out of an Asian ministry in Melbourne,
Australia, are strong in evangelism because it is practiced there as
a virtue and the ministry is led by Asians. It becomes a natural
expression of their faith in Christ.

Evangelism can prevent believers from becoming so
comfortable in the fellowship of believers that they die of spiritual
stagnation. Also, an accountable fellowship of believers can

prevent doctrinal diversion, falling into moral temptations, or gradually assimilating the world's value system.

Ephesians 2:19-20 summarizes the essence of our spiritual foundations: "Consequently, you are no longer foreigners and aliens, but fellow citizens with God's people and members of God's household, built on the foundation of the apostles and prophets, with Christ Jesus himself as the chief cornerstone." Regardless of the culture we are in, we are truly at home, and not aliens, when we are in Christ. He is the Creator of mankind and is establishing a supracultural Kingdom that is for the best welfare of men and women "from every tribe and language and people and nation." Colossians 1:16 teaches us that we are created by Jesus Christ and for Him.

E. Stanley Jones, a Methodist missionary to India, uses this analogy: "We fit Christ as a glove fits a hand." Christ-centered persons have divine resources to draw on to respond to life however they find it. They become salt and light in their culture. The sweet fragrance of Christ in them touches lives and helps them turn from "darkness to light, and from the power of Satan to God" (Acts 26:18).

OVERCOMING OTHER CHALLENGES

Given these foundational underpinnings, the returnee can draw on God's resources of grace, power, wisdom, and love to face the various challenges listed in the previous chapter. It is understood that change and adjustment take place gradually and call for patience. Let's look at some of them more specifically.

Weather

The temptation to complain can be overcome by recognizing that they have no choice in the weather; God has sovereignly ordained it. Therefore, to complain is to tell God that He is making a mistake. Praying will help give perspective, and giving "thanks in everything" is in obedience to the revealed will of God (1 Thessalonians 5:18). When we give thanks it is impossible to complain.

Traffic

I was traveling in Indonesia in 1988 visiting returnees with a dear American friend Steve, who was making his first trip abroad.

While being driven around Jakarta, he was rather nervous, periodically twitching in the front seat as he watched the chaotic traffic of cars, trucks, pickups, mopeds, and three-wheelers jockeying for another inch of forward or lateral space. He finally graphically described the dangerously close proximity of driving with, "They miss the paint!" (meaning they drive so close to each other without colliding). One could either see the negative aspect of the chaos, or one could give credit to how skilled the drivers were to survive this challenge day after day.

By learning Scripture portions such as, "Whatever is true, whatever is noble, whatever is right, whatever is pure, whatever is lovely, whatever is admirable—if anything is excellent or praiseworthy—think about such things" (Philippians 4:8), and praying them into our lives, we can practice them in the midst of chaotic traffic or any other situation.

Work/Career

The best training resource, in tandem with the truth of the Bible, is the role models of people who are already in situations that the internationals will be going into. Identify Christians in the workplace who are not only committed to honor the Lord in their work, but who are also giving their lives to making disciples of Christ. This is the outworking of *interdependence* (the student learning from the working layperson). The internationals will learn more from such people in a week than in four years of lectures. This experience will also broaden the vision of the layperson to include ministry in another part of the world through the international.

Two brothers, Herman and John, were profoundly affected by a few days of exposure to Wally, an active Christian real estate man in Minneapolis. They observed firsthand how he related to his wife and his grown children, and how he used his noon hours to exercise and minister to people.

How does a Christian businessperson operate without lying, stealing, and bribing as so many do? How does the professional make time for a devotional life and live in a godly manner when he works so hard? How does she do her evangelism? How does he find time to make disciples? A role model speaks more powerfully than any teaching the full-time Christian worker can give.

International Students, Inc., is in the beginning stages of a program called "Professionals in Partnership" that aims to match American Christian professionals with internationals in their field to provide mentoring and modeling. This will be very gratifying and has enormous potential. It is attracting professionals into this ministry that other means did not.

We can pass these principles on to the international students before they go home, thus better preparing them to make the adjustment back to their culture.

OTHER PRACTICAL WAYS OF PREPARING INTERNATIONALS FOR REENTRY

1. Encourage them to continue to use their own language while they are improving their English.
2. Foreign-language newspapers are in most university libraries. Encourage them to read them in order to stay in touch with their home country. If home country newspapers are not available, they can be requested from the librarian.
3. Lawson Lau, a Singaporean journalist, recommends constant correspondence with family (*The World at Your Doorstep*, InterVarsity, pages 108-109). He also advises obtaining free government publications from embassies to keep abreast of developments back home.
4. Help them get any Christian publications from home, even if they are just prayer guides.
5. During the last year before departure, help them develop their devotional life in their first language if they have not been doing this. Often there is resistance to this, but it is worth the extra effort in order to be better accepted back home. It is often embarrassing at a prayer meeting, say in Brazil, when everyone prays in Portuguese and the returnee prays half in Portuguese and half in English.
6. Help them memorize Scripture in their mother tongue.
7. Help them leave with no unresolved conflicts with people.

8. Recruit a few people to commit themselves to pray for the returnee. Have a photo and keep in touch by faxes, correspondence, an occasional phone call, or even personal visits.
9. Before departure, help them begin communicating with other returnees about job and fellowship possibilities.

The key issue is developing accountability at various levels. Help them establish contact with a home group, church, or Christian organization where they can be accountable to keep growing and ministering. Appendix A includes some organizations and individuals that can be contacted ahead of time to prepare for the returnee's arrival.

6
BUILDING
THE SUPERSTRUCTURE
Priority Issues of Reentry Preparation
✛

In light of the unique situations international graduates step into upon returning home, what are the priority issues, in addition to laying the foundations (chapter 5), that disciplers must pay attention to during their time away from home? Included are some specific ideas that could be used in mutual study and prayer. These are offered only as possibilities. It is hoped that disciplers will adapt them to fit themselves as well as the student. It is also hoped that these ideas will be launching pads for the development of even better resources.

An absolute minimum list of these priorities would include the following:

1. *Becoming a believer*

   ■ What it means to come to Christ
   ■ Assurance of salvation
   ■ Ability to explain salvation to nonbelievers

2. Development of a *growing relationship with Christ*

   ■ Christcenteredness in all areas of life
   ■ Devotional life
   ■ A lofty concept of God

3. An *overview of God's revelation* and essential truths of the Bible

    - Inspiration and authority of the Bible
    - Survey of the Bible
    - Essentials of interpretation
    - Foundational doctrines

4. Development of a God-given *mission vision*

    - God's redemptive plan and activity
    - World evangelization
    - Multiplying disciples

5. *Relating to parents*

    - Honor, respect and obedience
    - Sincere love
    - Witness by life and influence

6. Godly attitudes toward *materialism and money*

    - Ownership/stewardship
    - Motives
    - Eternal values
    - Ministry to the poor

7. Facing *temptation, opposition, and persecution*

    - God's victory
    - Satan's strategies
    - Love and perseverance
    - Moral and spiritual disciplines

8. Development of *godly interpersonal relationships*

    - Love, grace, mercy, wisdom
    - Servanthood
    - The fruit of the Spirit

9. Preparation for *marriage and family*

   ■ God's commands and principles
   ■ Role models

10. Preparation for *marketplace ministry*

    ■ Godly attitudes toward work
    ■ Exposure to role models
    ■ Role of laypeople

11. Identification of *how they have changed*

    ■ Who is the new person going home?
    ■ Potential conflicts at home
    ■ Strengths of the new person

12. Establishment of a *home-country contact for accountability and encouragement*

    ■ Identify possible people/churches
    ■ Correspond with them
    ■ Connect the returnee
    ■ Ask the returnee to make a commitment before the Lord to accountability

Whatever one's list of priorities, the implication is that during their stay here, *modeling, teaching,* and *experience* must be provided in these areas. This does not mean that the discipler must be strong and able in each of these areas. God has provided other gifted people, churches, and resources that can be drawn upon. Often the role of the discipler is to connect the right resources with the person being trained.

I would strongly encourage that the first step taken under any of the following topics be a simple Bible study on the topic. Later, supplement it with other materials, such as books, tapes, and videos, and people with firsthand experience. A book may seem overwhelming to an international in his or her senior year. But a one- or two-page study of God's revelation on the subject at hand has the advantages of being manageable and inexpensive, of developing the mind-set of first going to the Bible before other resources, and of being easily transferable to others. The following resources have proved helpful in each of the above areas.

BECOMING A BELIEVER

Out of a desire to maintain friendships with international students and not offend them, many Christians will not ask them if they come into the most important relationship in their lives. To ask is not manip- ulation, but a genuine dialogue that takes their eternal interest to heart. Even if the reaction is negative at that point, God can often use it to get them to consider the matter. I was a freshman international student in California in 1955 when I was questioned on this issue. Because I came from an Assyrian Christian background, at first I became angry and took it as a personal attack on my identity. But being challenged caused me to question if I was a real Christian from God's point of view. This forced me to be honest with myself and admit my need, and some weeks later I invited Jesus Christ into my life.

The problem is not whether we should ask students about their relationship with Jesus, but *how* we do it. If it is done in a proud, arrogant, holier-than-thou, judgmental attitude, then that's our problem. Neither is there any place for unethical practices of coercion or manipulation to induce people to respond to Christ. Sincere and honest dialogue is a sign of true friendship. The following five resources have proved very helpful.

Basic Christianity, John Stott, InterVarsity Press. Vintage John Stott addressing those investigating Christianity.

Jesus, based on the Gospel according to Luke. Multi-Language Media, Box 301 Ephrata, Pennsylvania 17522; (717)738-0582. This two-hour video has had a worldwide impact due to its availability in over 250 languages. It helps people overcome misconceptions about and get an accurate picture of Jesus. To enhance discussion and gradual assimilation, it is often used in sections rather than being shown all at once.

More Than a Carpenter, Josh McDowell, Tyndale. This is a standard college-level apologetic of the Christian faith by probably the foremost apologist among university students. I often suggest that the last chapter, telling Josh's spiritual pilgrimage story, be read first.

Symphony of the Universe, Chinese Christian Mission, Box 617, Petaluma, California 94953-0617; (707)762-1314. This is a scientific approach written by Chinese scientists, available in English and Mandarin.

The Storyteller's Bible Study, Bill Perry, Multi-Language Media, Box 301, Ephrata, Pennsylvania 17522; (717)738-0582. This study is designed to acquaint the student with the flow of God's revelation from Genesis to the Gospel of John. Perry has done this through the story rather than the doctrinal form for people with little or no biblical background, and because most of the non-Western world communicates truth by using stories.

GROWING IN CHRIST

A common challenge among those ministering to international students is how to disciple believers. Resources are available to help in being a host and a friend, as well as in leading people to faith in Christ, doing follow-up work, and discipling in general. But somehow these materials seem too conceptual, too mechanical (especially question-and-answer materials), or too Western in their cultural makeup or illustrations for internationals. Therefore, people are reluctant to use them.

I believe there is also a spiritual element involved here. Satan does not want internationals discipled to follow Christ as Lord and be equipped for ministry. So he gives us cultural" excuses not to use this or that material, and we end up frustrated, doing a lot of worship singing, having discussions, and getting speakers to address various subjects (as good and legitimate as these activities are) and call this discipling. But one of their greatest needs is to learn to discover God's truth from the source: the Bible.

One of the major questions we must ask ourselves in discipling believers is, What needs to be covered to give them the greatest benefit for a lifetime, and how can it be covered in a way that is suitable to their mind-set? One answer is that they must learn to love God's truth and experience ways of digging into the Bible to find what God has to say on any issue. When they are home and face the issue of corruption in the marketplace or government, how will they approach it?

If we have done our job well, they should be able to say, Let me see what the Bible has to say about this," and start probing, preferably along with their friends. That automatically implies that we have to teach them the use of a concordance or computer equivalents. It also implies that when they ask us a question, say about marriage, we should not give them our opinion or even a biblical answer, but say, Let's look together in the Bible to see what God has to say." This way the model of how to approach problems, questions, or issues is being set before them.

Actually, it is a good thing not to know which materials to use in discipleship training, as it forces us to ask, In the light of their going back to their culture, what is absolutely essential that they need to use back home?" What is thedare I use the term? *bottom line*? It helps to also ask, What did the early disciples have to work with?" I believe the answers are found in the book of Acts.

The early disciples were *filled with the Holy Spirit* (Acts 2:1-4; 4:8,31); and they met together for *teaching* (Bible), *fellowship* (love through mutual encouragement and sharing material needs), *breaking of bread* (worship focusing on Christ), and *prayer* (faith expressed in dependence on God). The result was *attractively changed lives*, *God's powerful working* through them, and *bold witness* in spite of persecution (Acts 2:42-47, 4:31, 8:2-4).

They did not have the *Design for Discipleship*,[1] *Quiet Time* booklet,[2] scripture-memory packets, prayer diaries, marriage videos, computer concordances, or *Four Spiritual Laws* pamphlets.[3] Yet Paul could tell the Colossian church that, All over the world this gospel is bearing fruit and growing" (Colossians 1:6).

There are at least two lessons for us: (1) we do not need extra biblical materials to disciple people effectively; and (2) we thank God for the materials we do have and use them until we create more suitable ones.

A missionary in Asia has come up with the following discipleship-training curriculum called the Three-Point Bible Study," for use with people in sensitive countries. It includes scripture memory, Bible study, and some topics essential to spiritual growth for young believers, replete with verses of Scripture. The only other item needed is a Bible in the person's language. The advantages of using such materials are their low cost, easy mobility, reproducibility, security sensitivity, and the ease with which they can be passed on to others.

THREE-POINT BIBLE STUDY

This is a simple method of written Bible study that will enable you to grow spiritually. As you study these basic Christian truths by short passages, you will get a grasp of important Bible teachings. This will prepare you to study whole books of the New Testament.

Because this three-point method requires no printed materials, you will find it easy to use in helping others begin Bible study.

The passages are primarily from the New Testament, since some people do not have an Old Testament. A few optional passages from the Old Testament are in parentheses.

As you begin each Bible passage, *pray*. Ask the Lord to teach you. Read through the passage several times. Think carefully about what it says. Then *write out* answers to the following questions:

1. What are *some main points* in this passage? (What does the passage say?)
2. What are *some main lessons and insights*? (What does the passage mean?)
3. What is *most helpful to me* in this passage? (How can I apply the passage to my life?)

Many passages take about one hour to study. Some can be done in thirty minutes. As you begin, study one passage each week. After you have studied several passages, you may want to increase your study to two or even three passages a week.

After you have studied fifteen topics with fifty-two passages, you will study the eleven paragraphs of Philippians 1 and 2. The book of Philippians is a joyful book that can help you become more Christlike. It is a good introduction to studying the books of the New Testament. Then after studying the four topics on being effective for Christ (Point D), you will finish Philippians.

Next you will study the rich books of Colossians (on Christ's supremacy and Christian living) and 1 Thessalonians (on living godly and expectantly). These studies will launch you into written study of the New Testament book by book.

If possible, find two or three others who would also like to study the Bible. After you have each completed your three-point study, meet for discussion of your studies and for prayer. This sharing together will provide fresh understanding and blessing. Or you may find it better to discuss two passages when you meet for discussion.

Second Timothy 2:15 is a great goal for your study of God's Word: Do your best to present yourself to God as one approved, a workman who does not need to be ashamed and who correctly handles the word of truth." And remember to pray as you study that the Holy Spirit will enlighten your mind and develop your life to be more like Christ's.

SAMPLE THREE-POINT STUDYJOHN 1:9-13

Some Main Points

1. The true light gives light to every person in the world (verse 9).
2. He created the world and its people (verse 10).
3. The people He had made did not recognize Him (verse 10).
4. His own people would not receive Him (verse 11).
5. Everyone who did receive Him became a child of God (verse 12).

6. We receive Him when we put our trust in Him (verse 12).
7. Those who trust and receive Him are born of God (verse 13).
8. This birth is a spiritual birth, not a natural birth. It comes from God, not from human descent or decree (verse 13).

Some Lessons and Insights
1. The person being spoken of in these verses is Jesus Christ (see verses 14-18). He is called the Word" in verse 1.
2. He gives light to each person in the world, but only those who receive Him become God's children (verses 9,12).
3. Most people do not realize who Jesus Christ is. Since He is the One who made them, and who wants to be known by them, this is a little surprising. Yet this resistance is by choice, partly because people love the darkness of sin (verse 10, also see John 3:19).
4. Believing" and receiving" Jesus Christ are the same thing. We become children of God with eternal life when we fully trust Jesus Christ as Savior and receive Him into our hearts (verse 12).
5. Verse 13 says that our spiritual birth doesn't depend on our trying to be a child of God. We also cannot receive it through our parents. No human being can make us God's child. Only God can do it. He does it when we trust and receive His Son Jesus Christ as our Savior and Lord.

Most Helpful Truth
This paragraph gives me assurance about being a child of God. My assurance depends on what God says. He says that He made me His child when I personally trusted and received Jesus Christ, and God cannot lie.

Tips on Using the Three-Point Study
1. Pages 52 and 53 are primarily for the discipler and do not need to be handed to the one being helped. All he or she needs is an explanation of the three points.

2. Page 54 gives an illustration of how to do the study and should be given to the young believer along with the list of scripture references below, or even small sections of it to get the person started.

3. Once the assignment is done, more references can be given out.

4. How you do the study with the person probably determines how he or she will do it with another person. The process is important because we want these studies to be passed from person to person.

A. *Know Jesus Christ*

1. God Is Great and Loving
   Acts 17:22-31What He is like
   1 John 4:7-12
   (Jeremiah 10:6-12)
   (Psalm 23)

2. Jesus' Birth and Humanity
   Luke 1:26-38
   Luke 2:1-20
   Luke 2:21-40
   Matthew 2:1-15

3. Jesus Christ Is God
   Luke 7:11-17Raises widow's son
   Luke 8:22-25Calms wind and sea
   Mark 1:21-28Expels demons
   John 5:19-29Powerful claims

4. Christ Died
   Matthew 27:1-26
   Matthew 27:27-44
   Matthew 27:45-66
   Romans 5:6-11

5. Christ Rose
   Matthew 28:1-15
   Matthew 28:16-20

6. Christ Promises the Spirit
   John 14:15-20,25-26
   John 16:5-15

7. We Are Saved by Faith

John 3:16-21
John 10:27-30
Ephesians 2:1-10
1 John 5:9-13

B. *Speak for Jesus Christ*

8. How to Share Your Testimony
   (Before, How, After)
   Acts 26:1-11
   Acts 26:12-18
   Acts 26:19-29

C. *Grow in Jesus Christ*

9. Grow in God's Word
   (Psalm 119:9-11)
   2 Timothy 3:14-17
   2 Peter 1:2-4
   2 Peter 3:17-18
   Luke 8:11-15

10. Pray
    Philippians 4:4-7
    Colossians 1:9-12
    Luke 11:5-10

11. Live Victoriously
    Romans 8:35-39
    Romans 12:1-2
    Hebrews 12:1-2
    Colossians 2:6-10

12. Do God's Will
    Matthew 7:24-27

John 14:21-24
James 1:22-25
1 John 2:1-6
John 15:9-11

13. Fellowship with Others
1 John 1:3-10
Acts 2:42
Hebrews 10:23-25

14. Tell People About Christ
Acts 4:8-13
2 Corinthians 5:18-21
1 Peter 3:15-18
2 Timothy 4:1-5
15. Grow in Christlikeness
Colossians 3:5-11
Colossians 3:12-17
Titus 3:1-8

D. *Philippians 1 and 2 Paragraphs*

1. Philippians 1:1-8
2. Philippians 1:9-11
3. Philippians 1:12-18
4. Philippians 1:19-26
5. Philippians 1:27-30

6. Philippians 2:1-4
7. Philippians 2:5-11
8. Philippians 2:12-13
9. Philippians 2:14-18
10. Philippians 2:19-24
11. Philippians 2:25-30

E. *Be Effective for Christ*

16. Let God's Spirit Control You
1 Corinthians 2:6-16
Romans 8:12-17
Galatians 5:16-21
Galatians 5:22-26

17. Flee from Sin
1 John 2:15-17
Mark 7:20-23
2 Timothy 3:1-5

18. See the World and Win Converts
Matthew 28:18-20

Acts 10:34-43
Acts 26:12-20
Matthew 9:36-38

19. Help Young Christians Grow
Ephesians 4:11-16
1 Thessalonians 2:10-12
Colossians 1:28-29
Acts 14:21-22

F. *Philippians 3 and 4 Paragraphs*

1. Philippians 3:1-6
2. Philippians 3:7-11
3. Philippians 3:12-16
4. Philippians 3:17-21
5. Philippians 4:1-3
6. Philippians 4:4-7
7. Philippians 4:8-9
8. Philippians 4:10-13
9. Philippians 4:14-20
10. Philippians 4:21-23

G. *Colossians Paragraphs*

1. Colossians 1:1-8
2. Colossians 1:9-14
3. Colossians 1:15-20
4. Colossians 1:21-24
5. Colossians 1:25-29

6. Colossians 2:1-5
7. Colossians 2:6-10
8. Colossians 2:11-12
9. Colossians 2:13-15
10. Colossians 2:16-19
11. Colossians 2:20-23

12. Colossians 3:1-4
13. Colossians 3:5-11
14. Colossians 3:12-17
15. Colossians 3:184:1

16. Colossians 4:2-6
17. Colossians 4:7-9
18. Colossians 4:10-13

H. *1 Thessalonians Paragraphs*

1. 1 Thessalonians 1:1-7
2. 1 Thessalonians 1:8-10

3. 1 Thessalonians 2:1-8
4. 1 Thessalonians 2:9-12
5. 1 Thessalonians 2:13-16
6. 1 Thessalonians 2:17-20

7. 1 Thessalonians 3:1-5
8. 1 Thessalonians 3:6-10

9. 1 Thessalonians 3:11-13

10. 1 Thessalonians 4:1-8
11. 1 Thessalonians 4:9-12
12. 1 Thessalonians 4:13-18

13. 1 Thessalonians 5:1-11
14. 1 Thessalonians 5:12-15
15. 1 Thessalonians 5:16-22
16. 1 Thessalonians 5:23-28

Now study Luke or Mark by paragraphs or half chapters, using the same three questions.

After Luke or Mark, try some shorter books. Perhaps:

1 John	1 Timothy
James	Romans
Galatians	

As you study these books you may want to try writing a brief title for each paragraph, and then use these titles to summarize or outline the whole book.

There is also profit in finding and recording one or two cross-references for each paragraph.

After these books, go on to study the Gospel of John by this three-question method. Then:

1 Peter	2 Timothy
Ephesians	2 Peter
1 Timothy	Hebrews
Acts	2 Corinthians

Continue on through the remaining nine books of the New Testament.

SIX ASSURANCES

The following six verses help young believers find security in their new relationship to Christ. Memorizing these scriptures will enable them to recall God's truths when in doubt.

1. Assurance of Salvation   John 3:16

2. Assurance of Eternal Life   1 John 5:11-12
3. Assurance of Forgiveness   1 John 1:9
4. Assurance of Answered Prayer   John 16:24
5. Assurance of Victory   1 Corinthians 10:13
6. Assurance of Guidance   Proverbs 3:5-6

SIXTY KEY VERSES

The following is a listing of *The Topical Memory System,*[4] a scripture memory syllabus that helps young believers establish strong biblical foundations in following Christ and serving Him.

Series A: Live the New Life

Christ the Center	2 Corinthians 5:17	Galatians 2:20
Obedience to Christ	Romans 12:1	John 14:21
God's Word	2 Timothy 3:16	Joshua 1:8
Prayer	John 15:7	Philippians 4:6-7
Fellowship	Matthew 18:20	Hebrews 10:24-25
Witnessing	Matthew 4:19	Romans 1:16

Series B: Proclaim Christ

All Have Sinned	Romans 3:23	Isaiah 53:6
Sin's Penalty	Romans 6:23	Hebrews 9:27
Christ Paid the Penalty	Romans 5:8	1 Peter 3:18
Salvation Not by Works	Ephesians 2:8-9	Titus 3:5
Must Receive Christ	John 1:12	Revelation 3:20
Assurance of Salvation	1 John 5:13	John 5:24

Series C: Rely on God's Resources

His Spirit	1 Corinthians 3:16	1 Corinthians 2:12
His Strength	Isaiah 41:10	Philippians 4:13
His Faithfulness	Lamentations 3:22-23	Numbers 23:19
His Peace	Isaiah 26:3	1 Peter 5:7
His Provision	Romans 8:32	Philippians 4:19
His Help in Temptation	Hebrews 2:18	Psalm 119:9,11

Series D: Be Christ's Disciple

Put Christ First	Matthew 6:33	Luke 9:23
Separate from the World	1 John 2:15-16	Romans 12:2
Be Steadfast	1 Corinthians 15:58	Hebrews 12:3
Serve Others	Mark 10:45	2 Corinthians 4:5
Give Generously	Proverbs 3:9-10	2 Corinthians 9:6-7
Develop World Vision	Acts 1:8	Matthew 28:19-20

Series E: Grow in Christlikeness

Love	John 13:34-35	1 John 3:18
Humility	Philippians 2:3-4	1 Peter 5:5-6
Purity	Ephesians 5:3	1 Peter 2:11
Honesty	Leviticus 19:11	Acts 24:16

Faith	Hebrews 11:6	Romans 4:20-21
Good Works	Galatians 6:9-10	Matthew 5:16

For those working with Mandarin-speaking Chinese, the following material (written in simplified script) corresponds exactly to the previous sixty key verses.

60个要点经文

基督是中心	A— 1. 林后5:17	2. 加2:20	
顺从基督	3. 罗12:1	4. 约14:21	
神的话	5. 提后3:16	6. 书1:8	过新生活A
祷告	7. 约15:7	8. 腓4:6-7	
交通	9. 太18:20	10. 来10:24，25	
见证	11. 太4:19	12. 罗1:16	

人人有罪	B— 1. 罗3:23	2. 赛53:6	
罪的刑罚	3. 罗6:23	4. 来9:27	
基督代付赎价	5. 罗5:8	6. 彼前3:18	传扬基督B
救恩不在行为	7. 弗2:8，9	8. 多3:5	
必须接受基督	9. 约1:12	10. 启3:20	
得救的确据	11. 约-5:11-13	12. 约5:24	

祂的灵	C— 1. 林前3:16	2. 林前2:12	
祂的力量	3. 赛41:10	4. 腓4:13	
祂的信实	5. 哀3:22-23	6. 民23:19	倚靠神的资源C
祂的平安	7. 赛26:3	8. 彼前5:7	
祂的赐给	9. 罗8:32	10. 腓4:19	
祂在试探中的帮助	11. 来2:18	12. 诗119:9，11	

以基督为首	D— 1. 太6:33	2. 路9:23	
从世界分别出来	3. 约-2:15-16	4. 罗12:2	
坚定不移	5. 林前15:58	6. 来12:3	作基督的门徒D
要服事他人	7. 可10:45	8. 林后4:5	
慷慨的捐助	9. 箴3:9，10	10. 林后9:6，7	
传福音	11. 徒1:8	12. 太28:19，20	

爱心	E— 1. 约13:34-35	2. 约-3:18	
谦卑	3. 腓2:3，4	4. 彼前5:5，6	
圣洁	5. 弗5:3	6. 彼前2:11	长成基督的样式E
诚实	7. 利19:11	8. 徒24:16	
信心	9. 来11:6	10. 罗4:20，21	
善行	11. 加6:9，10	12. 太5:16	

QUIET TIME

Phil Saksa of International Friendships, Inc., in Columbus, Ohio, has used the following format to help train young believers in how to develop a devotional life.

Objectives:

General   The person has a regular time when he has fellowship with God.

Specific
1. He has a daily quiet time.
2. He spends twenty to thirty minutes in his quiet time.
3. He follows a specific reading plan.
4. He prays following ACTS (*A*doration, *C*onfession, *T*hanksgiving, *S*upplication).

Content:

1. Show him *what* is involved.
   Scripture: Psalm 5:3 and 143:8
   Principle: Pray to God and listen to Him speak to me in the morning.
   Illustration: Jesus spent time alone with God (Mark 1:35).

2. Show him *why* he should have a quiet time.
   Scripture: Matthew 4:4

Principle:	Man needs God's Word to survive spiritually.
Illustration:	We need to have two or three meals a day to have physical strength.We also need to feed ourselves spiritually every day.

3. Show him *how* to have a quiet time.
   A. Practical illustrationsmethods
      Specific time, place, plan.
      How to meditate on a Bible passage.
   B. Get him started.
      Have a quiet time with him.
      Give him *Seven Minutes with God* pamphlet as a starter.
   C. Keep him going.
      Have other quiet times with him periodically.
      Share blessings you have received from your quiet time.
      Have him share his blessings with you.

4. Show him *how to pass it on* to others.

Scripture:	2 Timothy 2:2
Principle:	Blessings are to be shared, not stored.
Illustration:	The Dead Sea is dead because it takes in fresh water but does not let it out.

Quiet Time" can be taught formally or informally, depending on which approach the international responds to best. This simple exercise can be expanded as the student grows (for example, using the Psalms to illustrate a person's communion with God) and can be used to train others in how to do follow-up.

Following the Shepherd by Donald Wolf is another helpful follow-up pamphlet that can be used to help brand-new believers to begin growing. It is available from him at 3975 Willow Ridge, Holt, Michigan 48842; (517)694-8356.

Where there are no materials, create your own. All you need is the subject matter and the passages of Scripture (in context) that speak to the subject. Either individually or together, look at the passages, asking God to reveal His truth, and then discuss them together.

The remaining step in the growing-in-Christ process, after helping international students dig in the Bible for answers and direction, is one of obedience. This can be initiated by asking, In the light of what God is saying and my commitment to let Jesus be

Lord of every area of my life, what needs to change in my life so that He is in control of this aspect of my life?" Once the need is identified, ask, What steps will I take to bring about the change, and who will I ask to keep encouraging me to make these changes?" As part and parcel of the growing-in-Christ process, developing an attitude of humility is a high priority. The international graduates often return with attitudes of pride, arrogance, and superiority. The following methods could be utilized to train these students: *Bible studies* on the subject; *praying for a humble spirit*; and *discussing where this attitude might be presently manifesting itself*, as well as how it could show up back in their home culture.

Some passages to consider would be: *pride*Leviticus 26:19, 2 Chronicles 26:16, Psalm 10:4, Proverbs 8:13, Malachi 2:16, James 4:6; *humility*Deuteronomy 8:2, 2 Chronicles 7:14, Psalm 25:9, Matthew 11:29, Ephesians 4:1-3, 1 Peter 5:5-6.

AN OVERVIEW OF GOD'S REVELATION

God is holistic in all His dealings. There is always an overall plan, and redemption is no exception. Hebrews 1:1-3 portrays the process of His revelation. Therefore, the discipling process needs to include how the bits and pieces of God's revelation and plan for His creation fit together.

A very helpful overview of God's plan has been skillfully put together in story form by Bill Perry in *The Storyteller's Bible Study*, Multi Language Media, Box 301, Ephrata, Pennsylvania 17522; (717)738-0582. Each of the twelve chapters has teacher's notes, the actual study for students, and discussion questions.

While this study has been fruitfully used for evangelistic purposes, especially for those with no religious background, it is also a good way of grounding new believers in an overview of God's revelation.

Any of the Bible handbooks, such as Halley's or Unger's, have very helpful material on how the Bible was put together, brief summaries of each book of the Bible, and how God inspired the writers, among other topics.

MISSION VISION

The graduates who return home are inundated with pressures to prove their worth, please their parents, excel in their job, make all the reentry adjustments, marry the right person, and make lots of money. The primary pull is clearly in the materialistic direction. What will guide them in decision making? What will determine their value system? In short, what will they give their lives to?

If they have a clear vision of what God wants them to do, they will know their priorities and make decisions based on an eternal-value-system. If their mission isn't clear from the Bible and there is no commitment to do the will of God, they will drift in response to the strongest currents they face.

John R. W. Stott's article, The Bible in World Evangelization," in *Perspectives on the World Christian Movement*, edited by Ralph Winter and Steven Hawthorne, is an excellent six-page article to study with an international to help develop a world vision. By focusing on the Bible's mandate, message, model, and power for world evangelization, Stott helps us learn what is on God's heart and how to become participants in His plan. The book is published by William Carey Library, Box 128 C, Pasadena, California 91104.

RELATING TO PARENTS

This is a priority issue because the returnees will be relating to their parents the rest of their lives, because the Bible puts a high priority on the parent/offspring relationship, and because the returnees will be parents some day.

I have seen the results of how returning believers treat their nonbelieving parents. Those that are looked upon as pagan" and not respected and appreciated in the name of standing up for Christ" find themsleves in an adversarial role. Those parents who are loved, respected appreciated, and obeyed (to the degree that conscience will permit), are happy with their children and more open to their message. Many a parent, and even grandparent, has come to Christ because of the consistent testimony of their children.

In addition to Bible studies on the subject, two resources are very helpful.

How to Speak to Our Elders About Christ. This thirty-three-page booklet is very helpful to those Chinese whom Tay Mui-Lan describes as tongue-tied in dialects, unsure of our Chinese heritage, confused about the ideals of our Chinese elders, so that communicating the Gospel to them becomes a cross-cultural experience." This booklet can be ordered from:

OMF Books
10 W. Dry Creek Circle
Littleton, CO 80120   Tel. (800)422-5330
                                       (303)730-4160

Dear Mum and Dad is published by InterVarsity Press, 38 De Montford Street, Leicester LE17GP, England. The author, Chua Wee Hian, is the former general secretary of the International Fellowship of Evangelical Students. He draws from a worldwide experience of ministry to university students to help them honor their parents. He tackles questions such as how should we relate to our parents? How do we honor and obey them? When do we say, We must obey God rather than men"? How can we understand our parents so that we can openly communicate with them? How can we best share the gospel with our fathers and mothers?

MATERIALISM AND MONEY

In the spring of 1992, the Indonesian Christian Fellowship of Madison, Wisconsin, asked me to give a presentation on moneyhow to handle it during student days and after graduation in the home country. The study below is just one sample of a topical Bible study that anyone can create.

A CHRISTIAN VIEW OF MONEY

I. OWNERSHIP

   Everything comes from God and belongs to God1 Chronicles 29:10-17

II. STEWARDSHIP

God is saying, I trust you enough to let you have this money. Now put it to good use in line with My purposes."

To carry out this trust, God has established two major principles:

A. Attitudes

1. Faithfulness1 Corinthians 4:1-2
2. IntegrityActs 5:1-11 (4,8-9)
3. Generosity2 Corinthians 8:1-4
4. Sacrifice2 Corinthians 8:1-4
5. Cheerfulness2 Corinthians 9:7
6. Contentment1 Timothy 6:6-10
7. Humility1 Timothy 6:17

Upon returning you will find the pull of materialism is very strong. Therefore, develop biblical convictions.

B. Investment

1. GodMalachi 3:6-12, Matthew 6:19-21, 1 Timothy 6:17-19

Illustration: Hotel and department store in Singapore owned by a Christian. The store is closed on Sundays, yet continues to prosper.

How do you give to God? By giving to:

Those who minister to youGalatians 6:6
■ Church
■ Christian workers
■ Special ministries like Christian radio stations

Those who minister to others1 Corinthians 9:14
■ Mission agencies around the world
■ Children's ministries (e.g., Child Evangelism)
■ Prisoners' ministries (e.g., Prison Fellowship)
■ Ministries to prostitutes

Those in special need2 Corinthians 8:13-15

2. Personal/family1 Timothy 5:8
NecessitiesFood, clothing, shelter, health
DesirablesEducation, transportation, future
LuxuriesDo we really need a BMW instead of a Toyota?!

III. APPLICATION

A. What do I do with my money now?

1. Make a conscious commitment to look at your money the way God does.

2. Practice God's principles of stewardship.

   ■ Budgeting
   ■ Giving
   ■ Saving

   Remember 2 Corinthians 8:12, For if the willingness is there, the gift is acceptable according to what one has, not according to what he does not have." Therefore, don't feel guilty about what you cannot do.

B. What do I do with my money after graduation?

   1. Do the same thing you are doing now. The main difference is the amount.

   2. Special considerations:

   ■ Support of parents.
   ■ Support of education of brothers or sisters.
   ■ Investments to make in planning for future.
   ■ How to respond to needs and requests.
   ■ How to influence economic development for the poor.

   3. Ask for suggestions from graduates who returned before you.

The basic tools needed to put a Bible study together are a Bible and a concordance, or a topical Bible. List the pertinent passages and study them by asking these questions:

■ What is the main truth being conveyed?
■ What universal principles, applicable to any culture at anytime in history, are conveyed?
■ Are any definitions given?
■ What attitudes is God asking us to cultivate toward the subject?
■ What positive and negative illustrations are there in the Bible or in everyday life?
■ Are there any commands to be obeyed?
■ Are there any pitfalls to be avoided?
■ In what ways can I bring my thoughts and actions to reflect what God wants?

TEMPTATION, OPPOSITION, PERSECUTION

Anyone living the Christian life will face temptation. Some will face outright opposition to their identification with Christ. Yet others will be persecuted for following Him. Those returnees whose families are of a different religion often pay a higher price. The Bible is replete with illustrations of those who suffered for being loyal to the Lord (Noah, Joseph, Moses, Job, Jeremiah, Daniel, Jesus, Peter, and Paul, just to name a few). Church history is also full of brave men and women who faced fiery trials for their faith.

Dr. Everett Boyce's *The Challenge: Victory* gives valuable insight into the suffering church in Asia. It is available from ISI, Box C, Colorado Springs, Colorado 80901. It should be noted that this manual for Christians under pressure is being revised and updated.

There will be some cases where young believers will return to a part of their country where believers are nonexistent, or at least unknown. While rare in modern times, this situation can occur. What help can be offered these brothers and sisters?

We can commit them to God and to the word of his grace, which can build you up" (Acts 20:32). Granted, the Apostle Paul wrote that to the elders of the Ephesian church, but the truth of the Bible being a source of growth is still there. We can prepare them by looking into the Bible at people who found themselves alone like Joseph in Egypt (Genesis 3941), Elijah in the Kerith Ravine east of the Jordan River (1 Kings 17:1-6), and Daniel in a Babylonian lion's den (Daniel 7). We must also make a firm commitment to pray for them over the long haul, for we expect them to be faithful to the Lord to the end.

We can correspond with them, unless they inform us that it is detrimental to them. We should also learn from them what other security factors to avoid, such as negative statements about the state religion. Before they leave the country of study, other international believers who have been in the same church or fellowship should be encouraged to correspond, and if possible, visit them. Also, we should try to visit them in their country at their invitation. And when possible, they should be encouraged to visit believers outside their area or country.

Though they may not know of believers personally, through the networks of our organizations, particularly International Ministry Fellowship (see Appendix A), cautious use of known believers in the country, such as foreign diplomats or professionals, can be made. In many a capitol city there are international churches with believers from different nationalities. The returnees should not give up easily after a few tries without success. They should keep trying to relate to believers in the network. It is also crucial that the student makes contact with believers in the home country before he or she leaves the country of study. Meetings can be arranged outside the returnee's country before the returnee goes back in.

INTERPERSONAL RELATIONSHIPS

Because relationships are high on God's priority list, and because we live with relationships all our lives at home, in the workplace, in the neighborhood, and in the church, a biblical understanding of what is meant by Love your neighbor as yourself" is of the highest priority.

While studies or books on the subject could be found in a Christian bookstore, it is far more profitable to help the international create a study from such passages as Matthew 57, 1 Corinthians 13, Ephesians 45, and Colossians 3. This way the international experiences the truth of the proverb

If you look for it as for silver
   and search for it as for hidden treasure,
then you will understand the fear of the Lord
   and find the knowledge of God. (Proverbs 2:4-5)

In some social structures, people cannot afford expensive Bible-study books or even booklets. Therefore, if we teach internationals how to create their own studies, many more people can be served when they return home and pass it on.

In preparing a study on interpersonal relationships, the international should ask the following questions to the passages listed above:

- What commands are there?
- What principles are always true?
- What are the consequences of godly relationships?
- What are the consequences of ungodly relationships?
- What provisions has God made to enable us to relate in a godly manner?
- How do conflicts arise?
- How does God want us to handle conflicts?

Other more specific questions will arise from the context of individual passages.

MARRIAGE AND FAMILY

Together with your international friend, create your own Bible study on this subject. Use this as an occasion to teach your friend how to use a concordance in either book or computer form. There are three ways of doing this.

1. Look up words related to the subject, like *marriage, marry, husband, wife,* etc.
2. Once you compile the various teachings of Scripture, place them in categories, such as seeking God's will, courtship, parents' say in the matter, marriage ceremony, role of husband, role of wife, principles of child-raising, divorce, etc.
3. Study the truth conveyed in pertinent biblical stories, such as Hannah praying for a child (1 Samuel 12) and Eli and his children (1 Samuel 2).

Hui-Ming and Alice, of Malaysia, have been international students as well as effective cross-cultural missionaries among students for more than a decade. Their experience is that very early in the discipling process it is crucial to emphasize the importance of the teaching of 2 Corinthians 6:14, Do not be yoked together with unbelievers. For what do righteousness and wickedness have in common? Or what fellowship can light have with darkness?"

The dangers of violating God's standards and the blessings God intends with obedience should be discovered through Bible study, discussion, prayer, and commitment making.

At this point a simple study that points out the indicators God uses to help us determine His will would be very appropriate, as this is a lifelong need.

The videos listed below are recommended as study guides before the students go home as well as resources to take with them not only for their own use but also to help those they will disciple. The presenters are African-American and white North American missionaries with experience in Africa, Asia, and New Zealand. All videos listed are recorded in the NTSC format.

Dr. Tony Evans

Guiding Your Family in a Misguided World

Renaissance Productions
601 Mantua Pike, Ste. 200
Wenonah, NJ 08090   Tel. (800)234-2338
                              (404)943-3868

Elven and Joyce Smith

EJSO1	*Understanding Each Other* (67 min.)
	Love (52 min.)
EJSO2	*Friends & Lovers Through Life* (69 min.)
	Commitment (50 min.)
EJSX	Two tape setorder from:

Castle Bookstore
P. O. Box 6000
Colorado Springs, CO 80934   Tel. (719)594-2288

Jim and Jeri White

JJWO1	*Communication* (68 min.)
JJWO2	*Consideration* (28 min.)
	Personal Affection (38 min.)
JJWO3	*Gratitude & Affirmation* (68 min.)
JJWO4	*Leadership and Adaptation* (65 min.)

Acceptance (57 min.)

Order from Castle Bookstore (above).

While both videos and audio tapes are useful, there is no substitute for the real thing, living with a Christian family. Most international students we meet do not come from believing families and therefore have not experienced a Christian-family role model. When they have their own families, how will they lead them? They will do what their parents did. Consequently, it is of paramount importance that our discipling process includes as much exposure to believing families as possible. This may include periodic meals or outings together. It may include some weekends living with the family, especially during school-break times. It may include living with a family for a whole school term or year.

It is one thing to teach principles of family life from the Bible; it is another thing to see them lived out. It is in this context that deep, lifelong convictions are developed. At this point a sincere question is often raised: If they live with an American family, won't they pick up American culture that will work against them when they return to their culture? The discipler or host family can ask them to verbalize what they have been learning and how the application might be different in their own culture.

Mr. Lim spent just one week living with Kamel and Badia Shalhoub and their two girls in San Jose, California. The purpose was, within time constraints, to receive maximum exposure to a Christian family committed to love Jesus Christ and to help others love Him, too. Lim entered into every aspect of their lives—meals, family devotions, outings, entertaining guests, Bible studies, helping the girls with math, going to the Hewlett-Packard plant where Kamel works, and so forth. Lim came away with a liberal arts education in family life he could not get from books, audio or videotapes.

MARKETPLACE MINISTRY

There are several helpful works on a biblical view of work and ministry related to the workplace. Among them are:

Your Work Matters to God, Doug Sherman and William Hendricks, NavPress

The series on Ministry in the Marketplace published by Vision Foundation contains four booklets:

- *Your Purpose*God's universal purpose and unique purpose for each individual.
- *Why Go to Work?*What does eight to five, Monday through Friday, have to do with Christianity?
- *Whose Job Is the Ministry?*Biblical basis for the ministry of the laity.
- *The Profit Motive*Is there a relationship between reward in Heaven and motivation on earth?

These booklets are available from:

Vision Foundation
8901 Strafford Circle, Knoxville, Tennessee 37923
Tel. (615)690-4603, Fax (615)690-9322

Bible studies and books on working and ministering are more useful and help develop deeper convictions when augmented by personal exposure to people who are living out these principles in the workplace. Do you know people who are practicing these truths? Put your student friend in touch with them. Let the international spend a day at the workplace of your working friend if at all possible. The international will observe how this person goes about doing work, relating to colleagues, perhaps participating in a Bible discussion at lunchtime, or dealing with problems in a Christlike manner. This would be worth ten lectures on the subject.

Before returning to Indonesia with a master's degree in management information systems, Mr. Lim spent two weeks learning from business and professional people committed to making disciples in California's Silicon Valley. He lived with them, talked with them, prayed with them, studied the Bible with them, and went to work with them. It was a mini-mentoring experience.

I visited him in his family business six weeks after he returned and found him already putting into practice what he had learned. He told me that in order to spend adequate time with God in the city of Jakarta and do a good job at his father's business, he needed to get up at 5:00 a.m. This meant that he had to be in bed by 9:00 p.m. or so. I saw that as maturity and commitment.

He learned part of this from the example of Kamel, with whose family he lived for a week in San Jose, California, during his exposure to people ministering in the marketplace.

THE CHANGED INTERNATIONAL RETURNING HOME

Bible studies on the lives of Ezra and Nehemiah, who were aliens in the Babylonian culture and then returned to their homeland to serve God, can be developed.

Some questions to ask concerning the text would include:

- How long were they away from their homeland?
- What foreign influences were they exposed to?
- To what extent were they affected by these influences?
- To what extent did they resist being influenced?
- What motivated them to stay true to their God?
- Why did they return home?
- What was their vision for their homeland?

The first three chapters of 1 Peter address evangelism carried on by minority and displaced people. The formulation of the study could be done with the students as a means of training them in how to develop their own Bible studies.

Besides containing brief studies on Naomi, Moses, the Lord Jesus, and Paul, *Think Home*, a workbook by Lisa Espineli-Chinn, helps internationals discover how they have changed physically, socially, academically, emotionally, politically, financially, spiritually, and in purpose and ambition. For the table of contents of this workbook and how to use it, see Appendix D.

Another way of preparing internationals to handle reentry challenges better is to capitalize on their first cross-cultural experience by having them address the following questions:

- What challenges did you face when you first came to this country to study?
- How did you cope with these challenges?
- If you could do it all over again, with the experience and wisdom you now have, what would you do differently?
- As you anticipate returning home, what challenges do you expect to face?
- How will you attempt to handle them, given what you learned from your first experience?
- What spiritual, mental, and people resources can you draw on to help you?

ACCOUNTABILITY IN THE HOME COUNTRY

If returnees grew up in Christian communities, it is natural for them to return to them. If they came to Christ while abroad and came to know other believers from their hometown, those relationships can continue once they return. This puts a responsibility on the disciplers to find people from the same country and facilitate networking relationships. In Surabaya, Indonesia, some graduates of the University of Wisconsin are working with each other in the same business.

Appendix A lists a number of organizations that would be helpful in fostering networking relationships for fellowship and accountability in the home country.

SOME NOTES ON METHODOLOGY

After thirty-two years in ministry with students, I believe, while content is more important than form (methodology of communicating content), people copy what we do and how we do things. Therefore, it is important how we go about the discipling process. Jesus adapted His methods to His audience. He used several methods of communicating truth or training His disciples:

1. He spoke to the woman at Jacob's well (John 4) indirectly and tenderly at first, and did not violate her dignity in spite of her sinful lifestyle.

2. To some unteachable Pharisees He spoke in a very straightforward manner: You belong to your father, the devil" (John 8:44).
3. He taught mostly in the flow of life (for example, while in Zacchaeus' homeLuke 19:1-10).
4. He taught by design (Jesus did not want anyone to know where they were, because he was teaching the disciples"Mark 9:30-31).
5. He modeled ministering to people with the disciples watching (Luke 7:11-17).
6. The disciples experienced ministry firsthand and gave feedback when they were done (Luke 10:1-20).

Given the limited time we have with international students due to their demanding involvement with their studies, the material presented in this booklet can be passed on in a variety of ways:

- One-to-one agreed-upon regular planned times (for example, weekly) to fit both parties' schedules
- Group studies for groups of two or more
- At meals and other informal times
- At conferences, seminars, and training programs
- During longer sightseeing trips at school-break times

In the early stages, it would be helpful to focus on laying the foundations (chapter 5). The internationals are open to more specific reentry preparation material such as the *Think Home* workbook in the last six to twelve months before they leave for home.

NOTES
1. *Design for Discipleship* is a Bible-study series of six booklets on discipleship published by NavPress, P. O. Box 35002, Colorado Springs, Colorado 80935. Some internationals respond to the question-and-answer approach; others do not.
2. *Quiet Time* is a booklet on developing a personal devotional life by InterVarsity Press, Downers Grove, Illinois 60515.
3. *Four Spiritual Laws* is a small pamphlet that explains the essence of the gospel of Jesus Christ, published by Campus Crusade for Christ, 100 Sunport Lane, Orlando, Florida 32809-7875.
4. *The Topical Memory System* is a scripture memory syllabus published by NavPress, P.O. Box 35002, Colorado Springs, Colorado 80935.

7
VISITING THE INTERNATIONAL
A Unique Commitment as a Spiritual Parent

It may be difficult to conceive of a relationship between Thunder Bay, Canada, and Miri, Malaysia. But when I walked into the home of Thomas and Agnes Bang in Miri, I met a retired Canadian couple from Thunder Bay. When Thomas was a student in Canada, this couple had become so involved in his life that they had become Mum and Dad. The Bangs were delighted to have this couple come eight thousand miles to visit, encourage, and strengthen them, as well as learn from them.

Whether you were involved in personally helping your international friend consciously turn to Christ, or you were the primary spiritual pediatrician, having adopted a spiritual baby and parented him or her, you are looked upon as a spiritual mother or father. How the internationals look at you is more important than how you perceive them. One day Ramzi, who was on my ministry team at the American University of Beirut, introduced me to a friend of his as my best friend. It shocked me because I had no idea he thought of me in those terms.

If there is a bond between you and an international who regards you to be the spiritual parent, then no one can quite replace you. Our daughter Debbie married Rick and moved to Del Rio, Texas, which is about seventeen hours driving time from our home in Colorado. But both of them expect and look forward to my wife and me coming to visit them. Spiritual children also hope for those visits. Going to their home countries and visiting them in their homes has many benefits.

1. They are honored as well as encouraged to see a familiar face who played a special role in their lives while living away from home.
2. They are rightly proud of you before their parents and friends.
3. It gives them the opportunity of returning love and hospitality.
4. Their parents receive you with much gratitude for looking out for the welfare of their offspring when they were too far away to do so.
5. You are likely to have opportunities to witness to unbelieving parents and friends that few others will have.
6. You get a clearer picture of what their present needs are as a spouse, parent, professional, neighbor, servant of Christ, or church member.
7. You learn firsthand the realities of reentry and are in a better position to disciple other internationals when you return home.
8. You learn their daily life customs of greeting others, entering a house, eating, dressing, entertaining, and words and phrases in their language that can be applied with other students once you return home.
9. They can share struggles with you that they may not tell others.
10. You may be able to facilitate their entering helpful accountability relationships with other believers if they haven't yet done so.
11. If their vision or heart for God has waned, you can be used to help bring revival.
12. You can bring resources such as books, tapes, and videos to assist them in their ongoing personal, family, and ministry development.

13. You can learn firsthand about racial, religious, political, and social issues that the student may not have told you about in your country.

It takes a God-given parent heart to give yourself to them like this. Ask God to multiply your investment through them to all the nations. During the first few years of returning, internationals are so engulfed with the challenges of reintegration, career, marriage, children, and local ministry that they may not have the time or energy to think of a world vision. But as they settle in, a visit from you can help them open their eyes and look at the fields that are ripe for harvest. These returnees have already crossed cultures, learned another language, and adapted to a new way of life. They are people who take initiative and risks. This qualifies them to be missionaries outside their own cultures, either as tentmakers or even as traditional full-time workers.

As the spiritual parent, no one can take your place. A personal visit is well worth the time and financial investment. This is not intended to promote an unhealthy parental control relationship. Rather, having released them when they left the country of study, you demonstrate a kinship that is greatly appreciated by them.

8
HOME AGAIN
Help Available in Home Countries
✚

After graduating from an American university and participating in a short-term missions project in Asia, Eric returned to his homeland, Norway. At one point he wrote me a nine-page letter detailing the painful process of adjusting.

What help is available when international graduates return home? Some countries like Indonesia and Malaysia have a long history of citizens studying abroad and then returning home. The secular and spiritual friendships these people formed while overseas give them natural connections once they return. Others do not have these networks, making it more difficult for them to find help.

Christian internationals have two sources of fellowship when they return home: the local church, whether underground or open, and more informal fellowship groups. The local church has the following advantages:

1. It already exists and does not have to be formed.
2. It is usually indigenous, using the local language and cultural forms.
3. It offers a spiritual family, which is especially needed for those coming from nonChristian homes.

4. It may be an international church that uses English, thus being closer to what the graduate has come from. This kind of church serves as a transitional experience until the graduate has made the basic adjustment back to his or her culture. Though some returnees move to a "belonging" stage in their own culture, looking for opportunities of fellowship and service where the character is less foreign, in some cases returnees may be led by the Spirit of God to remain in an international church because of the missionary opportunities among various nationalities such a church offers. However, for the majority of returnees, the international church is seen as a transitional step.

5. In the larger metropolitan areas, some indigenous churches will have an international flavor because of the nature of Christendom today. There are outstanding Christian leaders from many nations, such as Dr. Stephen Tong, who have gained international experience from studying in seminaries or universities abroad or having spoken at international congresses. A large number of returnees in Jakarta attend the church Dr. Tong pastors. This kind of atmosphere makes the returnee feel more at home than in an Indonesian church in a poorer section of Jakarta, which attracts a different social set. It would take a high degree of commitment and conviction in vision for an international to join the latter type of church.

The second source of fellowship is groups supplementary to the local church, made up of people who identify with each other, having had similar experiences abroad as well as upon returning home. They can help new returnees at many levels because they themselves have traveled that road. They, too, have had to struggle with issues like job hunting, corruption, family relationships, and marriage.

The International Fellowship of Evangelical Students (IFES) sponsors groups such as the Graduates Fellowship in Singapore and Malaysia. Information about these and other groups can be obtained from InterVarsity Christian Fellowship, 6400 Schroeder Road, Box 7895, Madison, Wisconson 53707-7895; Tel. (608)274-9001, Fax (608)274-7882.

The Navigators in Indonesia minister to growing numbers of returnees through *The Marketplace Ministry*, which is mostly active in Jakarta, Surabaya, and Bandung. They focus on two groups—married and single returnees—and provide Bible studies, opportunities for further growth, leadership training, premarital and marital counseling, and ministry outreach. More information is available from The Navigators International Student Ministry, P.O. Box 6000, Colorado Springs, Colorado 80934; Tel. (719) 598-1212, Fax (719)260-0479. In Indonesia itself, information may be obtained from: Para Navigator, Jalan Dago Pojok 36, Bandung 4061, Indonesia; Tel. 62-22-81128, Fax 62-22-84539.

The aforementioned organizations are just a sample of the help that is available. Appendix A lists other sources of information about opportunities for returnees in various countries of the world.

9
CONCLUSION

Much more could be said on ministry to international students. There are other issues to cover with them that would help them be better prepared for the rigors of reentry as well as to serve Christ for a lifetime. This work has been kept short in order not to make this task seem overwhelming. You can help disciple the future leaders of the world by asking God what of this material to use at what time.

Use the resources suggested. Come up with your own. Discover others by asking people in the same type of ministry what they are learning. Change what you do, improve it, make it cheaper, adapt it to different cultures. Experience an adventure of faith by going to international students' countries and learning firsthand what they go back to.

Most of all, pray to the Lord of the harvest that He will use you to influence national laborers to be sent into the harvest fields of the world. You don't have to do it alone. Band together with people of like vision but differing gifts to make a greater impact.

God has been raising up laborers for Himself like Alan in Malaysia, Herman in Indonesia, Hiroshi in Japan, Han in Korea, Lin in Taiwan, Choon in Singapore, Helen in the Philippines, Samson in Kenya, Edith in Zimbabwe, Joshua in Nigeria, the Shastras in Senegal, Pedro in Mexico, Oscar in Venezuela,

Fernando in Argentina, Daniel and Esther in France, Henrick in Denmark, Hani in Jordan, and many others. Let us believe God will do this more and more for His glory.

APPENDIX A

Organizations with Opportunities Abroad for International Graduates

1. International Fellowship of Evangelical Students (IFES)
    55 Palmerston Rd.
    Harrow Wealdstone
    Middlesex HA3 7RR
    England   Tel. [from USA] 011-81-863-8688

    IFES contact in the U.S.:

    InterVarsity Christian Fellowship
    6400 Schroeder Road, Box 7895
    Madison, WI 53707-7895   Tel. (608)274-9001
                                    Fax (608)274-7882

2. International Fellowship of Christians puts out a directory
    of international churches that use English around the world.
    Information can be obtained from:

    International Ministry Fellowship
    134 Miramar Drive
    Colorado Springs, CO 80906   Tel. (719)576-7756

3. International Resource Ministries
    Campus Crusade for Christ
    100 Sunport Lane
    Orlando, FL 32809-7875   Tel. (407)826-2800
                                    Fax (407)826-2851

4. International Students, Inc.
   P.O. Box C
   Colorado Springs, CO 80901   Tel. (719)576-2700
                                                Fax (719)576-5363

5. The Navigators International Student Ministry
   P.O. Box 6000
   Colorado Springs, CO 80934   Tel. (719)598-1212
                                                Fax (719)260-0479

6. For information on churches, mission organizations, and Christian fellowships outside the U.S., contact:

   World Evangelical Fellowship (WEF)
   141 Middle Rd 05-05
   GSM Building
   Singapore 0718   Tel. [from USA] 011-65-339-7900
                                 [in Singapore] 339-7900
                      Fax [from USA] 011-65-338-3756

   WEF in Wheaton, Illinois   Tel. (708)668-0440
                                         Fax (708)653-8023

To get in touch with concerned individuals who will be happy to receive returnees, contact the above organizations. It is highly recommended that you write, fax, or call the receiving person about the arrival of the returnee, giving the returnee's address and phone number, asking the receiving person to contact him or her. In addition, your friend should also call the receiving person within a few days of being home.

APPENDIX B
Tips on Traveling to Visit Returnees
✤

1. *Take someone with you,* if at all possible. Companions provide strength and encouragement. They can be sounding boards and protection against temptation. You can also minister to more people. Whom should you consider as companions?

- Your spouse
- A fellow worker
- A business or professional person who has a ministry in the workplace

A note of caution: If you take an individual or couple for whom the new culture arouses much stress, it is embarrassing for your hosts and much energy goes into taking care of the "misfits."

2. *Start planning at least six to eight months ahead.* Flights to or from Asia can be heavily booked, especially in the summertime. I have found travel agents who are consolidators to offer more attractive prices.

3. *When possible, stay in the returnee's home.* Often this leads to witnessing to parents or relatives. It also gives you a better idea of what your friend is facing.

4. *Let the returnees know, before you arrive, of your gifts and the areas of ministry that God has blessed you in.* This helps them make plans for your visit.

5. *Don't panic if you get little or no communication from the other end.* Somehow it all works out. Just be sure you have up-to-date phone numbers and addresses.

6. Ask the returnees you plan to visit if there is *anything they would like you to bring.*

7. *Take gifts* like books, tapes, videos, Christian magazines, calendars, candy for children, or anything uniquely American.

8. *Be prepared to speak on very short notice.*

9. *Reconfirm ongoing flight reservations as soon after arrival as possible.* The airlines require reconfirmation within a minimum of seventy-two hours before departure, otherwise your booking may be canceled.

10. *Take family pictures*, as well as pictures of the international while he or she was on your campus.

11. *Recruit specific prayer support.* A prayer card with requests for each place you plan to visit is very helpful. Be sure to include a prayer for good health when you return, as your resistance will be low. Thank those who pray by sending a report after you return.

12. *Find out information ahead of time* about local currency and exchange rates, electrical voltage, plug adapters, weather, appropriate clothing, what food or water to avoid, and essential local customs. For example, shoes are taken off at the entrance of the house in most Asian homes. It is simpler, in such situations, to wear sandals or loafer-type shoes rather than the laced kind. This information can be obtained from international students, experienced travelers, or travel agents.

13. When possible, *have your returnee friends introduce you to others who are about to come to your country for further studies.* Put them in touch with caring Christians at their destination. The Association of Christian Ministries to Internationals (ACMI) has a program called Interlink that will help network new arrivals. They can be reached at: 7 Switchbud Place C 192-209, The Woodlands, Texas 77380; Tel. (713)367-5020, Fax (713)821-1329.

14. Sometimes, to *get a more accurate picture of the country you are visiting,* you may want to visit people you don't know, read local English language newspapers, or talk to people in the Christian community who are of a different background than your friends. All these will give you a better idea of what your friends face.

15. *It is cheaper to make overseas phone calls or send faxes from the United States to other countries* than the other way around. Making prearranged dates for family members to call you while traveling helps economize.

16. To conserve the lessons you learn about the trip, plus any reporting you may do, *take a little time each day to record highlights, observations, and insights.*

APPENDIX C
Recommended Books, Videos, and Audio Tapes for Returning Internationals
✛

Christian internationals should take home with them various reference books and other resource materials on foundational and priority issues listed in chapters 5 and 6. A partial list of helpful books and audio tapes follows:

BOOKS

Apologetics
Know Why You Believe, Paul Little, InterVarsity Press
More Than a Carpenter, Josh McDowell, Tyndale

Biography
Sadhu Sundar Singh, Moody Press
Shadow of the Almighty, Elizabeth Elliott, Harper/Collins

Career
Your Work Matters to God, Doug Sherman and William Hendricks, NavPress

The Church
The Church Unleashed, Frank Tillapaugh, Regal

Doctrinal and Devotional
Pursuit of Holiness, Jerry Bridges, NavPress
Spiritual Disciplines for the Christian Life, Donald S. Whitney, NavPress

Leadership
Be the Leader You Were Meant to Be, LeRoy Eims, Victor

Marriage
How to Be Happy Though Married, Tim LaHaye, Living Books
The Mystery of Marriage: As Iron Sharpens Iron, Mike Mason, Multnomah Press

Ministry
The Master Plan of Evangelism, Robert Coleman, Revell
The Lost Art of Disciplemaking, LeRoy Eims, Zondervan

Missions
In the Gap, David Bryant, Regal
Perspectives on the World Christian Movement, edited by Ralph Winter and Steven Hawthorne, William Carey Library

Reference
A concordance to match their Bible translation
New Bible Dictionary, Tyndale
Tyndale New Testament Commentaries, Tasker, Eerdmans
Unger's Bible Handbook, Moody Press

Some of the above titles can be bought for reduced prices from:

1. Moody Generic Editions
    Moody Press
    820 North LaSalle
    Chicago, IL 60610   Tel. (312)329-4000

2. CB Distributors
    Box 3687
    Peabody, MA 01961-3687   Tel. (617)535-6400

AUDIO TAPES

Bible teaching (especially book by book) by:

Chuck Swindoll	Insight for Living Box 69000 Anaheim, CA 92817	Tel. (800)772-8888
Charles Stanley	In Touch Ministries 777 W. Peachtree St. NW Atlanta, GA 30308	Tel. (404)347-8500 Fax (404)347-8549
Warren Wiersbe	Good on topics. Available from: Spring Arbor Distributors Box 985 Belleville, MI 48111	Tel. (800)395-5599 Fax (800)395-2682
Home/Family	Back to the Bible Box 82808 Lincoln, NE 68501	Tel. (800)395-5599 Fax (800)395-2682

APPENDIX D
Other Resource Materials on Reentry
✤

Lisa Espineli-Chinn's workbook, *Think Home*, addresses many of the issues raised in this book. It is available from ISI, Box C, Colorado Springs, Colorado 80901. It combines biblical and practical insights. It is designed for self-discovery for individuals as well as small groups. The table of contents is listed below.

User's Guide
Chapter 1: Why Are You Returning Home?
Chapter 2: Your Life in the United States
Chapter 3: Who Is Going Home?
Chapter 4: Your Experience with Christ
Chapter 5: Developing a Spiritual Support Group
Chapter 6: Reentry Bible Studies
Chapter 7: Evaluating Your Ties Back Home
Chapter 8: Who Is Back Home?
Chapter 9: Welcome Home!
Chapter 10: Potential Reentry Problems
Chapter 11: Tough Questions
Chapter 12: Growing Spiritually Back Home
Chapter 13: Serving God Back Home
Chapter 14: Closure and Packing
Chapter 15: On the Plane
Chapter 16: Settling In
Reentry Reading List

In addition to the "User's Guide" in the workbook, here are some tips on how to use this tool: Both internationals and disciplers need to make a commitment to study it and have the discipline to stay with it week after week. Begin the study six to nine months before they leave for home. A good time is during the winter break when they are bored and not distracted by their studies. After graduation and before they leave is a good time for debriefing and review, so that the issues and principles are fresh in their minds as they go home. Look upon repetition as a positive factor.

The Christian in the Chinese Culture. Poh Boon Sing, a Chinese Malaysian, wrote this to help first generation believers understand, relate to, and share Christ with their families and friends. Sometimes readers need to evaluate the author's strong personal views with grace and maturity, but Chinese students here in America and graduates abroad who have read it find much that has been very helpful. The book can be ordered from:

Good News Enterprise
106, Jalan BS 5/3
Taman Bukit Serdang
43300 Seri Kembangan
Malaysia

Church and Culture. This book, edited by Bobby E. K. Sng and Choong Chee Pang, is a compilation of eight scholarly presentations given in Singapore in 1991 by Singaporeans addressing the relationship between the Christian faith and indigenous cultures. This book will probably find a more welcome response from Ph.D. or postdoctoral students. Though it is not as practical as I would wish, returning internationals need to read what those who have struggled with the issues have written. It can be ordered from:

Graduates Christian Fellowship
420 North Bridge Road #05-05
Singapore 0718

"Preparing Effective International Returnees" is both an insightful and practical paper by Dr. Alvin Low of Malaysia and Singapore, who is presently working with the A.D. 2000 and Beyond movement. For more information contact Dr. Low at 850 Wycliffe Drive, Colorado Springs, Colorado 80906. Tel. (719)576-2000.

The World at Your Doorstep. While the whole book is helpful to those ministering to international students, chapter 7 focuses on "Preparing for Reentry." Lawson Lau and his wife, Pam, from Singapore, have been international students. Because Lau is a professional journalist, reading this book is all the more pleasurable. The book is available from InterVarsity Press and is under consideration for revision.

Members of the Association of Christian Ministries to Internationals follow the National Association for Foreign Student Affairs (NAFSA) Guidelines on standards for community groups.

It is expected that ACMI members will share their faith with internationals. However, this dialogue is to take place in a spirit of mutual respect for the other person's beliefs and practices. Furthermore, coercion or manipulation is not to be used to change the religious beliefs of the international student.

The views expressed by a particular ACMI member do not necessarily reflect the views held by the membership at large nor the ACMI Board of Directors.

Johnny Tatum
ACMI Executive Director

AUTHOR

Nate Mirza grew up in Iran and India before coming to California as an international student. He came to know Jesus Christ personally at Cal Poly, San Luis Obispo, California. He and his wife, Kay, served with The Navigators in India, Lebanon, and Iran for fifteen years. Since 1977 they have been working with international students in Wisconson and Colorado. Nate is a graduate of the Near East School of Theology in Beirut, Lebanon, and one of the founders of the Association of Christian Ministries to Internationals (ACMI).

Since 1988 he has made five trips to Asia and the Middle East to understand what international graduates of overseas universities face when they return home. He has developed relevant strategies to better prepare these students for more meaningful integration in their home cultures and fruitfulness in God's Kingdom.

He is presently the co-coordinator of The Navigators International Student Ministry. The Mirzas have two daughters and a son-in-law.